INTIMACY

men and their love relationships

OLIVER FREEMAN

G
P

Intimacy
paperback ISBN 978 1 76109 910 6
ebook ISBN: 978 1 76109 913 7
Copyright © text Oliver Freeman 2025
oliverginfreeman@gmail.com

Published 2025 by
GINNINDERRA PRESS
PO Box 2 Bentleigh 3204
ginninderrapress.com.au

For Susie who, single-handedly, got me over the line and for Liz and Gill who did their best in trying circumstances.

'What are men going to do to help themselves break out of patriarchy and come into a new system where they get free to be tender, loving, caring, heart-opened, feeling beings?'
Eve Ensler

'Bigamy is having one wife too many. Monogamy is the same.'
Oscar Wilde

CONTENTS

Poems

Foreword

BY WENDY McCARTHY AO

Oliver Freeman has seven children, from three marriages, and, at the time of this publication, will have 17 grandchildren.

He has a deep personal experience of love and marriage that he hopes at long last has set him on a rewarding course and hopefully for those around him too.

He says that some of his reasons for writing this book are that he now understands that "Men have been assuming something close to ownership of their female partners and spouses for as long as we can remember; now the demand for freedom is on us.

"The outing of the behaviours of celebrity and powerful males is confirming the evidence on which this demand is based. There is much more to come. Our institutions – the police, the church, sport, education, business, and government among them – have a systemic bias to protect their own at the expense of the rights of women, not to mention children."

He thinks he has something worthwhile to say.

A contrary view is that some people might think after three marriages he might not have much of value to say about love and marriage

It would be easy to say Well hello! About time ! Just another recidivist man seeking redemption.

But it is not so simple. Oliver does have something to say and has chosen memoir and poetry as his genre as he writes about his life, loves, failures and successes. He is taking a risk and invites us to walk in his shoes.

And isn't this what we said as young emerging feminists in the 'sixties and 'seventies as we invited young men into our lives to learn to live and love differently? We wanted marriages/relationships between equals and that love must include respect and intimacy.

As the author of two memoirs, I have found it a satisfying genre and believe many of us practise the craft of autobiography in our inner intimate conversations with ourselves about the meaning of our experiences. Few of us set about writing. Yet it is the commitment to the story telling of our lives which helps us make sense of them and the setting in time helps the contemporary reader see where they fit.

Critics of memoirs (usually your immediate family!) dismiss them as vanity but it is a particular way of making sense of one's life by exposing, sharing, and owning it warts and all.

Oliver has chosen to be vulnerable as he reflects on

a long life where the definition of what it is to be male has shifted. He examines his life through the lens of an older man very aware of the social changes in his lifetime.

I hope men will follow his journey and find the joy of equal and intimate relationships.

I am writing this Foreword not only by invitation but also because Oliver and I have lived in a similar universe although I am two years older and can claim seniority. Given the times it was surprising to discover that we both went to preschool which undoubtedly gave us a headstart in life. This could account for some of our precocious behaviour later.

We met in late 1986 at the wedding of Bettina Arndt and Warren Scott and have been friends ever since. There were lots of connections, Oliver had been on the cover of Forum, where I had articles published on adolescent sex education. These were provocative actions for the times.

Tina's father had taught Economics to my husband Gordon at ANU. Gordon and Oliver had both worked in publishing and other businesses. Strangely both had been engaged with the promotion of The Female Eunuch by Germaine Greer, Oliver in England, and Gordon in Australia. Both loved the book which immediately gave them some feminist credibility,

In the 'seventies and 'eighties *Family Planning* and *Forum* magazines were important sources of community information about sexual health. Tina edited *Forum* magazine which was owned by Penthouse magazine and was variously described as an erotic and /or educational magazine which featured letters, articles on health medicine and psychology, and social relationships not all of which were erotic. It had a substantial readership.

It was a publishing initiative which titillated and informed and was likely to attract interests from publishers like Oli and feminists like me working in sex education.

We first met as guests at her wedding and agreed that we would find a restaurant for a late meal. Oliver the Englishman took over, to find the right place probably in recognition of his role for the last couple of years as author of *Cheap Eats in Sydney*. He had done a lot of eating out! By the end of the night this little group of people had moved into what I would call fast intimacy, that feeling that you could trust and share stories and dreams with the people at the table. It doesn't happen often. We came home feeling happy and I remember saying to Gordon I think Oliver and Susie are always going to be our friends.

Over the years, we have stayed in touch in what I would describe as a personal professional friendship which included birthdays, special celebrations, new business interests. and shared work opportunities always within a trusted friendship. These relationships have their own intimacy where sex is not part of the agenda and we can feel secure that we can work without being harassed. During the time that I have known Oli we have worked on many projects. And I am not sure that he knows this, but he has the capacity to create a trusted working environment which is a very particular skill.

By the end of the 21st century we could probably say that most couples no longer lived as part of a large family or community where there are extended networks to confide in, to feel at home with, to trust and mentor and we often expected a lot of our partners. We expected them to provide more of the emotional needs than a larger community once might have done.

Oli describes true intimacy as the great provider and destination for what starts as romantic love which he now believes is unsustainable. He mourns the lack of males who want to discuss this with their partners or other males.

I do too.

When we met Oli was on that journey and about to be married for the third time. I was mildly intrigued as my experience of marriage was different but marriage is a broad church and I have long believed that it is best not to examine other people's relationships. Oli and Susie were so obviously happy and committed to each other and wanted their relationship to thrive and flourish as it has. That is something to be celebrated.

I instinctively believed that the best relationships were between equals. I could see few examples of marriages that could work for me. I learned that the best marriage would be enhanced by a stable, nourishing, loving and intimate relationship. Our marriage was strengthened by feminism despite the dire warnings from men and women that my actions would destroy romance. It liberated us to share more of the responsibilities of everyday life and acknowledge that even in the darkest days you know you don't want to lose the intimacy and commitment

Oli has a gift for friendship and lunch and conversation. He has a curiosity about how the world works which is contagious. His work in scenario planning was ground-breaking. He was already reading the future. I had done some scenario planning in 1980 at a conference, but it was Oliver's thought leadership that lifted me into new insights and understanding and dare I say it the intellectual intimacy and friendships that many professional women were seeking -without the sex.

Female friends who worked with Oliver enjoyed his company and intellect. He is a great and natural storyteller who could lift you out of prosaic thinking and enable you to change and reimagine the issues.

I hope readers enjoy and appreciate this book as much as I have. It is a plea for kindness, friendship and trust and invites men to be more vulnerable in their relationships as Oli has been.

As poet Mark Tredinnick so eloquently writes it is presence not stardom women want in their lives and maybe a new script for men seeking intimacy.

And the poetry is an additional gift.

Wendy McCarthy AO

INTIMACY
men and their love relationships

INTRODUCTION

This book has been written with its focus on men engaging in love and sexual relationships that may span their lives, disrupt an existing relationship or be a bit of fun where the 'now' outweighs any thought about what happens next – not to mention the impact of such events on the exigencies of family life in a world full of stress and conflicting demands.

The book is part memoir and part a conversation on the social context in which we make these relationships. It includes poetry, mostly mine, which I find has such an acute link with the emotional life which relationships, in my case, may reveal. Achieving a balance between my 'big picture' reflections and my own autobiography has been hard but I trust I have been successful enough to make the enterprise of interest to readers outside the circle of my family and friends.

Above all I am driven by the knowledge that, in my world, day-to-day communication among men about the topics I cover is unusual. I am sure, for example, that most men masturbate, have accessed pornography or had affairs but we rarely talk about these things with each other.

Of course, the way we communicate with each other is largely a cultural phenomenon. I was born in the sepia world of the Second World War, raised in the yellow smog that typified the late '40s and '50s, discovered the psychedelic rainbow of the '60s before engaging with the multi-coloured palettes that followed.

The rocky road of feminism which for me took such an abrupt turn with the publication of *The Female Eunuch* has reached a new crisis point today with the revelations of the behaviours of men in power – especially in the media, the church, education, domestic and geo-politics – often abusing their positions by creating and exploiting opportunities to come onto their male and female victims in an institutional environment, whose first instinct seems to be to protect the perpetrators and ignore the victims. And we can add to these 'estates' family life, whether in the nuclear family or blended families, in which the private social boundaries often enclose a terrain of abuse and despair.

I was a member of the team that published the first edition of Germaine Greer's book. I have learned that one contribution to the mess that men find themselves in, is a general failure to understand the true nature of intimacy between the sexes; the idea that intimacy is the sex act itself rather than the character of a relationship across all its domains – gender, family, business, friendships, domesticity, society and so on – and across all times.

This book is unusual not as a personal account of how I discovered true intimacy in my love relationships but because I have written the book about my experiences with the male reader in mind. I do not see myself as 'holier than thou', far from it as I have lived a flawed life, but I do want to reflect on males and masculinity in contemporary society.

At its core, this is a book about how I have been able to transform myself from an arrogant, pleasure seeking, egotistical elitist middle-class white male into someone just a little less noisy, who appreciates the wonderful nature of true intimacy and the joys it has to offer.

I want to share and discuss with you what I have discovered about men and sex as a learning experience. Men are going through a profound sea-change at the moment and should embrace the uncertainty that it brings in the hope of creating a better future for themselves.

Beside the personal journeys that we make in our love and sex relationships there is the broader social journey being made by the cultures in which we live, whatever part of the world of which we happen to be part.

I do not take a view as to the role of social media in these events or the legal proceedings which have or may yet review the behaviours of men like Harvey Weinstein, Louis C K, Don Burke, Woody Allen, Rolf Harris and Bill Cosby.

I do, however, take the view that the endemic mess we find ourselves in is primarily a socio-political one and not just a matter of individual male psychology. Aristotle argued that men and women are social animals. What is often considered inherent or natural is actually learnt. Therefore, promoting socio-political change is the hardest challenge. The disruptive shift that is required is, by its very nature, not an organic or 'natural' development.

Institutions, whether they be Anglican or Catholic churches, private schools, corporations, governments, political parties or families, resist change to such a degree as often to deny the basic human rights of the people in their care.

Unfortunately, we – writers and readers – have little chance of facilitating the social changes that are needed to make institutions ethical and accountable for the behaviour of their members, so the fulcrum for action reverts to each of us to reflect on the way we live our lives, to learn from that reflection, and to communicate our learnings to others. And, maybe, even change ourselves!

Please note that I use the word 'marriage' to denote a permanent relationship between adults. However, I make no apology that my experience is almost totally heterosexual and that I have little to offer on the complexities of same sex or the recently emerged concerns with 'trans' relationships.

Reflections to one side – writing what is essentially a memoir is fraught with difficulty as this poem argues.

Unremembering

In the museum of my brain
Archives of remembering
Piled like logs ready for the fire,
Flamed by random kindling, is this mortal pyre
Flammable again, again and again?
That tickling table in the playground
My first kiss, sweet Yvonne
The day I refused apple fool
A mild dawn in the kibbutz school
With today's apples strewn around
Look at Liz dancing the stomp
As Georgie Fame pounds the keys
Addison's walk on May Day
When young voices from the Tower play
Fractured memories, a colliding romp
But it's a motor-psycho nightmare
Whose sinews stretch back through time
Connecting Susie, my children and friends
Along a road with unseen bends
And pills and urgent healthcare
The synapses are losing their spark
It's hit and miss, 'what was her name?'
Bricks of autobiography crumble and fail
As if my memories have been sent to jail
And mortality a hammerhead shark
In the recesses of my brain
I am losing archives of remembering.
The kindling basket full to the brim

But the logs won't light, the fires dim,
Unremembering, as memories drain
Not once but again and again

ROZELLE, 2017

Not to worry! After all it's only by living our lives that we learn how to live the life already lived.

Playlist

. . . .

Bing Crosby, Oh, What a Beautiful Morning
Marvin Gaye, Sexual Healing
Sam Cooke, A Change is Gonna Come
The Platters, Remember When
Georgie Fame, Yeh! Yeh!
David Bowie, Life on Mars

1

FOUNDATIONS

Protest

Bob Dylan sang about World War 3
A prescient voice it seems to me
As Trump and Hanson, May and Le Pen
Gather their troops, mostly men.
Nick Cave sang 'Go tell the women we are leaving'
But has he forgotten there is life after grieving?
It is time for the women to pick up the reins
And take us somewhere new – to feminised plains.
Perhaps to the world of Linda Burney
The things that have mattered on her journey
A world of grace and love, equality for all –
A tide that is turning; a new wrecking ball?

BONDI, 2017

It was early summer in London in 1970. Edward Heath had just replaced Harold Wilson as PM and the popular young kid Tony Jacklin an English golfer won the US Open. I was living in Dulwich and travelling each day to Granada's London offices – a welcome relief from the bland McGraw-Hill offices in Maidenhead which had been my first employer for the last three years.

The inscrutable, great and sadly late, Sonny Mehta, then editor of Paladin Books, came into my office in Upper James Street, Soho, around 4 pm and plonked the galley proofs of a book on my desk. 'Let me know what you think,' he said in his normal cursory manner, and left.

Six hours later, I turned the final page. I was spellbound. I knew this was something so special that I missed my usual 6 o'clock pint at the John Snow pub in Broadwick Street, just a platform shoe and flowery shirt away from Carnaby Street. Here was a transformational challenge, not just to the women Germaine Greer was aiming at, but to the men who, effectively, ran the world in which her analysis played out.

It was one of those moments rarely experienced by

publishers, when a book comes out that will change the way we see ourselves and each other. During my 50 or more years in publishing, nothing compares in my professional experience to the impact of Greer's book other, perhaps, than Henri Charrière's *Papillon* in the same year and, on a purely egotistical note, when Arthur Koestler, in 1973, selected a book I had just published (John Beloff's *Psychological Sciences*) as his book of the year.

Nevertheless, my involvement with *The Female Eunuch* was slight, of course, as UK sales manager for the initial hardback edition published under the MacGibbon & Key imprint. As my colleague of later years, Richard Neville, observed two decades later, I was after all about the fourth person in the world to read the book.

In those days, the creative 'trade' publishers of general fiction and non-fiction were purveyors of hardback books which tested the market for their later potential as 'cheap' editions i.e. paperbacks.

The book was hard to categorise. It wasn't cookery or gardening, biography or fiction, self-help or memoir. But there was something going on in the ether. I sensed this and went out on a limb by asking our press cutting agency to send me daily news clippings on the subject of women and society. The fat envelope they sent me each day confirmed a groundswell of interest in what was to become the women's movement. There were other writers like US authors Betty Friedan and Gloria Steinem kicking the new feminist ball in the park and attracting notice, but none gathered the audience, excitement and influence of the feisty Australian academic and part-time lecturer at Warwick University, Germaine Greer. She was offering an explicit call to action for a movement that had not yet fully started. She was, literally, creating the future with what became a great network of radicals from her involvement with *Oz Magazine, Suck Magazine* and *Private Eye*.

In 1970 she was way ahead of the curve. It is no surprise that I struggled, as a 26-year-old sales guy for Granada Publishing's hardback imprints, to get the attention of my colleagues. I had suggested to my boss, Jim Reynolds, that a first printing for the MacGibbon & Kee hardback edition should be 10,000 copies which was, briefly, entertained by the whole publishing team. However, on my return from a sales trip to Scotland (searching for both new book sales across the board and, to pacify my colleague Campbell Black, to experience a pint of Aitken's Heavy), the nervous publishing committee had reduced my suggested 10,000 to 5,000, of which only 2,500 were to be bound up for the initial sale. It was to be a hardback bound in a two-colour fluorescent pink and black typographical jacket – just about the cheapest two-bob production possible.

We launched the book at Ronnie Scott's Jazz Club in Frith Street, Soho, in October 1970 with the pre-publication sell-in to bookshops (fondly known as 'dues') standing at only 1,500 copies. The W H Smith

Book Club had turned me down and W H Smith's full-price scale-out of copies to their retail shops was minimal. Engaging with W H Smith could be confronting. I remember going on a sales trip to Harlow – a new town in Essex with only one bookshop – and failing to get the spotty youth buying books that day to order any copies of *The New Town Story* by Frank Schaffer. I was so angry at his rejection that I tore up the rest of his order and drove home vowing never to act as a sales rep ever again.

In those days, an estimate of total sales for a new book was about twice the number of sales on publication day. This suggested a maximum sale of 3,000 copies for *The Female Eunuch*, validating the revised print run and the puny advance that Sonny Mehta had negotiated with his fellow Cambridge graduate, Germaine.

Defying those predictions and what we thought we knew; the book went ballistic. The hardback sales galloped ahead with several reprints and, surprise, surprise, a very healthy book club sale. The market was clearly readying for the publication of the Paladin paperback with its wonderful 'torso on the washing line' cover by John Holmes just six months later. Germaine's book is still in print, selling annually well above the average sale for new books, and has been translated into over a dozen languages.

Soon after the success of *The Female Eunuch*, I attended a celebratory dinner at the Spanish Club in

London's Swallow Street with my boss, pipe-smoking Jim Reynolds, whose reputation was built on his publishing *Peyton Place*, our Granada Sales Director, Geoffrey Howard, and Humphrey Wilson, the owner of boutique publishers Crosby Lockwood, on whose acquisition, by Granada, I had spent the previous six months. Their list included gems like *Natural Poultry Keeping*, *Plants of the Bible* and *Adventure Playgrounds*.

Crosby, as it was called in 1800, then owned the rights to a novel by Jane Austen called *Susan* but failed to publish it. It appeared later as *Northanger Abbey*, published by John Murray. Crosby was, thus, one of the first entries in the now familiarly long list of publishers missing the best-seller boat. Granada, itself, was no exception turning down *Love Story* and *Jonathan Livingston Seagull* during my time. More recently *Harry Potter* was rejected by more than a dozen publishers before Bloomsbury said 'yes' and went on to make millions.

Back to the dinner, you could hardly expect three middle-class, middle-aged Englishmen and their 26-year-old male flunkey to spend much time debating Jane Austen, whose world view was so focused on the domestic and social world of middle-class women in another time. But we did debate at some length the institution of marriage.

My three co-diners had eight marriages between them; and Geoffrey had even married the same woman twice. 'The worst bloody decision I ever made,' he confessed. Jim and Humphrey were less phlegmatic but I challenged them. I had been married but once, and was still married to Liz, my childhood sweetheart, with three kids and living happily in Dulwich, anticipating a steady and settled future in London.

'Surely,' I argued, 'the drive to remarry is about you and not a negative judgement about your spouse. So, if you can't change yourself, then why change your spouse?' The benign smiles around the dinner table from the three wise men told me that I was missing the point and the conversation moved on to wine, football, cricket and other male preserves.

Now, almost 50 years later, I am writing this book about my publishing experiences and my relationships in my study in a pretty weatherboard worker's cottage in Rozelle – an inner-west suburb of Sydney. If you had told me on that evening in Swallow Street that I would become an Australian citizen, spending more of my life in Sydney than in London, I would have laughed you out of court. And if you had added, too, that my three marriages, seven children, 17 grandchildren, two sustained extra-marital affairs and a handful of fleeting one- or two-night stands, then, just maybe, the lad in the Spanish Club would have seen the conversation with Jim, Geoffrey and Humphrey as a learning experience rather than one held with waspish aliens from another planet.

A focus for my 'memoir' unfolds.

Playlist

. . . .

Edison Lighthouse, Love Grows (Where My Rosemary Goes)
Tommy Roe, Dizzy
George Melly, You've Got the Right Key But the Wrong Keyhole
Freda Payne, Band of Gold
George Harrison, My Sweet Lord

2

GROWING UP

Directive

Fall beneath the lowering moon
Arch your back in sharp despair
Let the shadows nudge your mystery
Sink into your senses' snare
For you know that I'm coming there

LASHAM, 1963

EARLY DAYS

I was born prematurely at around 32 weeks on Christmas Eve 1943. For the first two years, I had a rough ride. I was a very slow developer and was not properly weaned until I was two. I had pneumonia and my undiagnosed eye problem (congenital nystagmus or 'eye-wobble') meant I tilted my head to better see and this attitude was accompanied by an open mouth from which lolled an unusually long tongue.

This constellation of effects led me to be labelled a mental defective on my first medical records. No doubt, in an earlier time I would have been institutionalised in Bethlem or some god-forsaken place for the socially peculiar.

I did, however, attend the local Day Nursery School from the age of 8 months, so my learning development in the hands of institutions started about as early as possible.

Nursery school ended when I was five and my parents were unsure of my suitability to attend 'normal' school and decided to send me to Pinewood School in Ware – about 10 miles from Cheshunt where we lived. You might feel there is something strange to select a school so far away when you had neither car nor money to support the travel challenge. I never asked my parents 'why?' and, if I had, I am sure the answer would have been accidental to any sense of a plan.

The Pinewood story is for me about June the conductress on the green double-decker number 310 bus, which ran from Enfield to Hertford via Cheshunt. She was my first 'new' love.

There was a warmth to June which drew me to her. I used to wait for the bus this side of the Rose & Crown pub and cross my fingers that June would be on duty.

I rode this bus for two years on my way to and from Pinewood, a school for maladjusted and special children in Ware, Hertfordshire (my peers included Peter Kenyatta the son of the Kenyan leader, Jomo, and a young Angela Pleasance, daughter of the actor, Donald Pleasance). It was run by Miss Strickland – always known as 'Stricks' - a circular woman who wore voluminous Kaftan style dresses to hide her girth and, as I learned later, a bottle of Booths London gin. She had pebble glasses and messy hair in a bun and was no competition for June in my search for a surrogate mother.

Of course, I had a real mum at home but she wasn't much use to me when I was travelling to and from school on the bus, a trip of over 10 miles through Turnford, Wormley, Broxbourne, Hoddesdon, Rye House and Great Amwell. On my own. Aged five.

I will come back to June in a minute. But first, I need to tell you a little more about Pinewood and why I went there.

As I reflect back 70 or so years, it still strikes me as a very odd place to send a little boy on his own after such a fragile entry as mine into this world.

At the end of my 10-mile trip, I got off the bus by the canal stop and crossed the road. A busy main road. Then I ran by the greyhound kennels, attended by frenzied yapping and the fear that they would escape and eat me up, before opening the gate at the bottom of an enormous ploughed field which ran steeply to a wood, Pinewood, and on into the sky. There was a track across the field and when I reached the top, a stile for me to clamber over and into the trees.

The track was now rocky and wet with dense bracken and the smells of rotting timber, fungi and leaf mould. It was always dark in this nightmare of a place and I climbed as quickly as I could to reach the safety of the clearing in which the school stood. I expect the journey to the top was quite short but its darkness must be as vivid today as it was back then.

The return journey was much trickier for me during winter because it was getting dark at about the time I left school. I hurtled down the track, jumped the stile and continued running across the field before slowing so as not to disturb the dogs.

Then on to the bus and back home.

On one of the return journeys, on which my Dad happened to be travelling, the bus stopped at the Canal but I was not waiting to get on. A regular schoolboy, noted this, looking out of the window and announced, to the guffaws of his friends, 'the frog is not with us today!'

—

June was never on the returning bus. Just in the mornings. And when I saw she was on the bus, I glowed. She would sit me on the bench seat next to the platform for getting on and off the bus. The platform was where she stood between stops after she had done the tickets and from which she would ring the bell. Above her head set into the wall was a special shelf into which she put her clipboard of tickets. And next to it was a small lockable cupboard with her bag and carry-on items.

The bench was high so that her face was only a little bit higher than mine. How I loved to look at her. She had black curly hair (a perm I now imagine), the bluest eyes, red lips and pinkish make up. She had a very curvy figure and was every inch a woman despite the 'maleness' of the trouser suit uniform.

I was intrigued by the big button she wore with her number on it and the rack of tickets which hung from her neck – different colours for different prices plucked as needed from the rack and then punched to show they had been used.

When the bus arrived at Hoddesdon clock tower, over half way to Ware, June would step off the bus and nip into the greengrocer's just there and buy me an apple. This was the best piece of fruit I had ever had – every time!

After several months of meeting June, I became brave and decided it was time for June to meet my family. So, I summoned up the guts to ask my real mother if my stand-in mum could come for tea.

I was disappointed when she said 'no'. An implacable negative. And after another week or so, I let the matter slide from view.

Thirty-five years later, I recounted my passion for June to my mother and asked if she could remember why she had said no to my proposed tea party.

'Of course,' said my real mother, 'we couldn't ask

June to tea because she was a prostitute.'

No doubt June's apple was from the Garden of Eden.

Much later I wrote this poem about Pinewood:

School Days

I am a schoolboy now.
(greyhounds yap at me in unison from
    their chicken-wire kennels
flooding the air with anxiety, lost calls for action)
Taking the path away from the road
    and into the corn field
almost ready for harvest as July days shorten.
I am a schoolboy now.
(the corn shakes its husks at me,
cabbage whites and grasshoppers
    dancing in attendance)
The satchel sits awkwardly on my back
thumping the top of my bum as I gather pace
I am a schoolboy now.
(ferns swaying, the smell of fungus, mulching leaves,
and moss filling my nose)
Opening the wooden gate
I clamber a more private path into the wood
I am a schoolboy now.
(the plaintive call of a pigeon echoes through the trees
as a pheasant rises with a flapping squawk
    in the field just left behind)

My fear rises too as darkness shrouds the way
and my footfall fumbles on the rocky path.
I am a schoolboy now
(how much longer until I reach the heavy oaken door
and the safety of the school house
    at the top of the hill?)
Pinewood, a school for maladjusted children,
stands aloof from the journey I have made.
I am five years old.

ROZELLE, 2017

After Pinewood, I went to a co-ed primary school, initially Burleigh then Gews Corner school and was happy
to avoid the Pinewood journey. I certainly fancied some
of the girls (especially Yvonne in my class) but access
was tough because boys and girls were separated into
different playgrounds. I did manage to kiss 10-year old
Yvonne by crossing the frontier onto the girls' netball
court and was severely teased by the boys for so-doing.
I suppose it was a bit of a public kiss with 100 or so
kids cheering me along, as we rolled about on the playground floor, so I got what I deserved.

    I was of the opinion that girls were a different spe-
cies from us boys and the school regimes did nothing
to change that view. The view was culturally-based. My
experience of my own children – especially my young-
est family – has pointed to a different conclusion that
we are, in fact, all the same – male and female – and
that friendships without sex are as important as those

with. The 'different-same' continuum has been at work throughout my life with Simone de Beauvoir in *The Second Sex* locking me into one extreme (that women's biological role transforms their differences from men) and the quest for equality and fairness at the heart of the movement kicked into being by Dr Greer.

There was, however, one theatre for me that was quite different. Until I was 15, we lived in Cheshunt, a drab north of London suburb about 10 miles from Tottenham up the A10 towards the much prettier Hertford. Despite being mentioned in the Domesday Book, Cheshunt's claims to fame were slight; Henry V111's Cardinal Wolsey Anthony Trollope, the Victorian novelist, and Cliff Richard, the late fifties pop-star. I was briefly at school with Cliff (alias Harry Webb), though about three years younger and only 150 years younger than Trollope, author of the Barsetshire Chronicles who had worked in the local Post Office.

Our house was the end of a terrace of ten Victorian houses and we rented it for the princely sum of £1 then £1.50 a week. My memory of the place was reawakened 50 years later by Michael Frayn's novel *Spies* which seemed to have been set in a north London location just like this. Even the plot of his novel reflected a childhood fantasy of mine about the local Masonic Hall being a coven of German spies.

My upstairs bedroom window looked out over the front garden of 20 Mount Pleasant, Turners Hill, Cheshunt. On the opposite side of the main road was an entrance with a drive going up to a distant building. The entrance pillars were made of stone with an arched cast iron lintel announcing the name of the property, Halsey Masonic Hall.

The Halsey Hall Lodge had been consecrated on 29th September 1925, 18 years before I was born in Reading when my mother was on holiday.

Walnut Tree House is a large building and had two and a half acres of ground and a main road frontage of laurel. The Masons bought it for £3,500.

The land on which the house sits was to the north of Theobalds Park. We used to visit the Park by walking down Theobalds Lane with its blackberries and woods especially to admire the stuffed tigers and lions and to compare the cats with our tiger skin which our grandfather, Reginald Bocquet, had brought back from India.

The Park is also the home of historic Temple Bar, once the western gateway into the City of London at Fleet Street. It was at the edge of the woods and always surprised. Here was our Angkor Wat and we were the monkeys.

I was fascinated by the toing and froing at *The Lodge*. During lengthening summer evenings when the natural light to read by had gone, there was enough yellow light from the lampposts for me to see the men arriving in their black Austin and Ford cars and on foot. The walkers each had a small brief case and I wondered what could be in them – maybe, sandwiches or books or even important letters?

In the winter there were many more cars and I became focused on the yellow headlights, when the evening across the way had finished, which swept across the far wall of my bedroom to the left or the right if they were going towards Turnford or Waltham Cross.

The Lodge was forbidding. Although my parents had moved with my sister Sally to Cheshunt from Chingford in the early part of the war, brother Dan and I (thick as thieves) who were born in Cheshunt, never once ventured a toe past the entrance to *The Lodge*. It was a foreign land.

My bedroom at this time was reached through the family bathroom. Not so much an 'en suite' as a 'bien-venue à tous'. The bed ran along the window. It was a tall narrow black iron-framed affair and I managed with skilful use of a covered bolster, to position myself so that I could see across the road to *The Lodge* while keeping my head horizontal on the pillow.

Leaving time was more exciting than arrival as it all happened at once. The silence of the street after night-fall was broken by cars rattling down the drive, leaving their headlight imprint on my wall and taking their occupants off to their homes.

I spent hour after hour fantasising about these men (I never saw a woman go up the drive). What were they doing in there? Were they relatives of some famous person? It could be a restaurant, I supposed, but not a hotel because I never saw people leaving in the morning.

Then one day, when my wobbly eyes were tired of

reading, I came to a dramatic conclusion. After all, the war had only just finished. They were Germans! The cases contained German uniforms and secret documents which they had stolen from Cheshunt Town Hall. They were planning a new invasion of our country. It would need a lot of planning because their army had been captured. They would need hundreds of people already in Cheshunt to spearhead an attack on the Town Hall and the Library so that their much reduced invasion force could link up with them to overthrow the Mayor and his Aldermen.

'Donner und blitzen!' as my comic would say, 'der Englisher ist ein schweinhund!!' Well, maybe so, but the mystery of Halsey Masonic Hall was a fervent intrigue for me in my little world.

On Tuesday evenings at about 7.30, my imagining would be broken by a rap on our side door. Voices drifted up the stairs and I could make out those of John and Pat Horner who were regulars.

John was a trade unionist, later a Labour MP, with a big red face bearing several prominent moles, two of which sprouted hairs. I loved him. Flying down the stairs, I would bound into his arms, to be greeted by 'evening comrade!'

The mysteries of the Masons meeting across the road were, in retrospect, eclipsed by these everyday activities in our house as the local cell of the Communist Party gathered for another weekly meeting. But, you know, I knew that the events in our house were quite normal. It was those guys over there who were really spooky!

These were probably the most formative years of my life.

—

My dad taught me how to cry when listening to music. How to be overwhelmed by the arrogance of Beethoven and the moodiness of Sibelius in combining the romantic and the masculine in their violin concertos, by the divine melancholic nostalgia of Elgar's cello concerto or, again, by the Hegelian march of god on earth given to us by Hegel's compatriot, Richard Wagner, in the *Ride of the Valkyries*.

We had very little in the way of reproductive equipment. There was an old-fashioned wind-up gramophone treasured for playing strange songs –'*Susanna's a funny old man*', which being somewhat precocious I thought referred to 'Cezanne' as a fanciful man', the English folk song – *Buttercup Joe*, sung by Albert Richardson – and, a little later on, my first purchased record, Lonnie Donegan with his skiffle group on the *Rock Island Line*.

More important was a wooden upright steam radio, I remember most for its Monday night broadcasting of *The Goon Show* ('he's fallen in the water'- again), for *Toy Town* and *Children's Hour* in which David Davis' soft voice still resonates 60 years on and, of course, on Saturday mornings when Uncle Mac was a must-listen broadcaster with his Children's Favourites – special to me for Burl Ives, Danny Kaye, the Runaway Train and the Teddy Bears Picnic.

The radio was of every day importance. *Take if From Here* with the Glums, *Twenty Questions* with Gilbert Harding, the Archers (but why did Grace need to die in the stable fire?) and of course the two stalwarts of adult music choices – *Family Favourites* with Jean Metcalfe and the indomitable Roy Plomley with his *Desert Island Discs*.

'So what?', you may ask in the age of the Internet, of Facebook, Instagram, YouTube and iTunes. Haven't we got it better?

Well yes most of the time. We are clearly better off. None of my twenty-four children and grandchildren have had to go to school with no dinner money because there wasn't any. Or lived for several years without running hot water. And in a house with no car nor TV.

Their life expectancy is greater by a whole generation than mine when I was born in 1943. And tertiary education is more likely for them than not, as well as the ability to travel beyond the local bus stops and train stations.

I defy any contemporary of mine living in London and its environs in the '50s not to share positively most if not all the highlights of BBC Radio (Home, Light and Third Programmes) that I have listed in this memory bubble. Like a recent summer when I was in France travelling the Yonne river and canal with my eldest son Tom and his family when we encountered a narrow boat called *The Wilfred Pickles*.

I chatted to the owners on the river bank who were from Yorkshire and about my age. As we parted I said 'Give 'im the money Mabel' – a direct reference to the radio show, *Workers' Playtime* with Wilfred Pickles and his wife, which went out three times a week from a worker's canteen somewhere in the UK lunchtime. They were gobsmacked. As they made way, they called 'You're the first person we have met on our travels who knows who Wilfred Pickles is.'

This somehow gets to the point of difference between us traditionals and baby boomers and generations x, y, next or what. Our community, despite its hardships was just that – a community. When we listened to the Top Twenty radio program on a Sunday or, watched David Jacobs at Mr Wade's (the grocer who had a TV!), presenting *Juke Box Jury* – we were all sharing the same thing whether it was *Peggy Sue, Rubber Ball* or *Move It*.

We shared the same movies at cinemas with just one screen and sourced the same books from the Library next door.

This was a world without pluralism in all its different shades. Where multiple music genres were unknown that is beyond Pop, Jazz, Blues and Classical. And when everyone knew their place in a highly stratified social environment.

The ubiquity and singularity of culture strengthened our sense of community but it came at a price.

Access to higher education was limited, the class system inflexible and politics dominated by the grey old men, whom I will talk about soon.

Twenty years later, when I was living in Goldhurst Terrace, South Hampstead, a torrential storm created a flash flood which saw all the basement flats flooded to the ceiling and ground floor flats awash. Gill and I, fortunately, lived on the first floor but were soon helping our less fortunate neighbours to bale out their houses and providing them with blankets and towels, Scotch and beer.

Later in the evening we all fetched up at Peter's pub for a restoring ale. Ruby a spritely 70 year-old who had lost her cat and a goldfish in the flood, confided in me that despite her sadness 'I haven't had so much fun since the Blitz'.

At the back of the gardens of our Cheshunt house was a field stretching the whole length of the terrace which became the territory of the children living in these late Victorian houses. Apart from the three of us (me and my siblings Sally and Dan) and Val next door, there were eventually the 11 children from the Knight family two doors up (Valerie, Carol, Maureen, Joyce, Norma, David, Robert, Patsy, Sandra, John and Peter – give or take the odd failed memory!), and only child Angela about halfway down the street towards Waltham Cross. When school days and rain were absent, the field was fully in use, with Bonfire Night a special occasion every November 5.

We spent many an afternoon and weekend playing sports and tag activities which would often end up in bundles of kids on the grass. This turned out to be an excellent moment to cuddle any available girl and do a bit of exploration before the bundle moved on. We also had daring moments in the disused stables at the bottom of our garden when we'd challenge each to display our genitals on the basis – if you show me yours, I'll show you mine.

Despite the lack of money, my upbringing was rich in conversation and the arts – books, paintings in particular; being next to a public library was a god-send. Bohemian friends of my parents were frequent visitors and a source of entertainment for me. And every now and then I'd escape with Bernie, who is still my best friend 60 years later, to London town a bus-ride away.

The Hostage

Bernie and I are on the 715
'Finsbury Park' 'Manor House' 'Wood
    Green' 'Camden Town'
From the BBC, a short walk to Shaftsbury Avenue
Where The Hostage is playing.
Two kids sourced severally from
    Poland and White Russia;
France, Britain and Spain –
Engaging the drunken bombast of the borstal boy,
Barmy Brendan from Dublin

Carving a space for ourselves with our few shillings –
Tasting the danger of the big city
    and learning how to play.
A modest event just then
But now, overheard conversations, eavesdropping
Twelve thousand miles and 50 years later
As I write in Pearl Beach
Our singular channel had further reach
Sharing our experience of Dublin and the dead
Were those two poets, Sylvia and Ted.

Pearl Beach, 2003

THE PARENT TRAP

The short poem opening this chapter was written when I was 19 years old; a fully-fledged male keen to explore matters of sex. What strikes me about the poem now is how, without malice aforethought, it asserts that heterosexual sex may be prejudicial to the freely assertive female and emphasises what I feel is one of the great ironies about sex – that it is often an invasive act by the male, exploiting the female by entering her body. From a male point of view, the sex act carries with it many significant undertones – among them feelings of anger, violence and rejection. It's not surprising that commentators like Andrea Dworkin have argued that sex can be an expression of male contempt for women. The poem is, also, assuming that I am in charge and able to control my environment – some deceptive and erroneous thoughts as my life to follow proves.

I don't think my father, Frank – who was born way back in 1901 – ever gave up womanising. He was no role model for the conventional male idea that you should seek wide experience before settling down in a monogamous relationship with your life-long partner. He spent his life secretly playing the field.

Frank loved women and was a dreadful flirt; aspects of his life that rubbed off on me to but only to a degree. But what I learned positively from him above all else was to be both open-minded and disinhibited in matters of sex and love. I matured as unlaced rather than strait-laced, no mean feat in the pre-'60s universe. I was always shy when the idea of broaching my feelings came to hand but my partner of the last 40 years complains that I have no filters on the way I live and relate to others and I can now see how this may have affected my relationships. Always ready to go without much thought about the consequences. The extraverted optimist rather than the introverted cynic. Don't worry. It'll be alright! . . .well at least for me!

My mother, Pamela, took a much more conventional approach to relationships than my father. Loyal and steadfast she rode the waves and was remarkably patient with a very difficult, self-centred man. Looking back on their early lives, I am struck by the challenges they both inherited as middle-class children being weaned in the British colonial system. Their parents lived respectively in the West Indies and India and Frank and Pamela were each bundled off to boarding schools in England, staying with aged aunts, relatives and friends during the holidays. These were staid unstimulating environments in which to grow up but that is what they were given without any discussion or room for manoeuvre.

As a result, my parents had no experience of family life – as either siblings or parents – and were totally ignorant of their parents' relationships with each other. My mother was an only child, going to Upper Chine school on the Isle of Wight and Dad might as well have been an only child as his three brothers and sisters were brought up in the West Indies, while he attended an English public school, Christ's Hospital, in Horsham, Sussex.

Their experience of childhood clearly impacted on the way they brought us up and on our emotional lives. The Pinewood story illustrates the bizarre consequences of their attitude to parenting.

It is ironic that Dad's funeral in the Isle of Wight in 1988 was so sad not just because he had died but because of this failure to achieve his potential. My mother's funeral, twelve years later, was a more joyous event. We celebrated, among other things, her courageous life and shrewd intelligence, despite the dreadful social and personal faux pas for which she became famous.

An example of the latter was when visiting me in Australia, she joined me in my bookshop – Legal Books in the centre of Sydney town – to meet Glennis our bookshop manager. She then recounted to Glennis how she'd met Charles Hammick the prominent UK book-seller of that time who said his reason for bookshop success was that he only hired graduates. Glennis had left school in New Zealand at the age of 16!

The name of the ferry that took me from Portsmouth to the Island for her funeral in 1999 was, of course, *The Lady Pamela* – a newly conferred social status she would have adored! In contrast, the sadness already mentioned at Dad's funeral, 12 years earlier, was exacerbated by the visit my brother and I made to see him in his coffin at the undertaker's parlour before the service. The shrivelled old man's mouth was set, open-mouthed, in a noiseless scream in horror of a world that had let him down. This image reappeared recently when Susie and I visited the Edvard Munch Museum in Oslo and stood in front of *The Scream* – a surprisingly small canvas. How great paintings (music and texts) worm their way into your personal life, is one of the pleasures and surprises of engaging in the arts. And the other is how surprisingly small they can be – the *Mona Lisa* for example.

The impacts of their upbringing on their development as parents and role models for their children, are very interesting to me. My father never talked to me about his childhood. My mother did a little more but there was no family content. And it is not surprising that I have no memory of being positively cuddled by her although I do remember vividly stroking the back of her stockinged legs while sitting on the floor at her feet in front of the fire.

There was, thus, little 'touching' in my relationships with my parents and I don't remember seeing either of them naked. It is not surprising that I have no memory of meeting my surviving grand-parents on either side, although apparently, when I was three or four, I threw an alarm clock at Eugenie Blanche Sheppard, my great-grand mother from Jamaica. My sister Sally was not much of a cuddler either though Dan and I made up for it in the way little boys do – punching, hair-pulling and wrestling, not to mention synchronized masturbation as puberty between brothers just 17 months apart took hold!

A major consequence of the circumstances of our family life is the sense that my parents were not ever-present. During the '50s we had no money, no car, no TV, never dined out and it was up to us to invent our daily life, largely on our own. My Dad never came to sports events (well once) to watch us play and took a scant interest in the fabric of our school environment. We did, however, play cards as a family – initially Racing Demon and, later, when we had some loose change to buy chips, Draw Poker. Chess and Scrabble also featured. My other family memory is how we always ate together at our dining table with who sits where pre-ordained, as was the setting and clearing the table when finished.

They did show some interest in the careers of their children and . . . in my case, Dad prepared the text for a book on nautical sayings in the English language and literature as well as poems that he described as being 'anti-poems' so as to sit neatly next to TS Eliot and Ezra Pound!

Mum in addition to her botanical illustrations also responded with a plan for a text called *Curious and Clever Plants* which died an early death with my leaving England for Australia.

These general observations about my parents and family life should not obscure the fact that they loved us. I never once doubted their feelings. But the way your parents love you is clearly patterned, in turn, by their experiences as children. This in turn patterns our personal development – in many cases to be mastered and overcome; in others to be cherished and built on. And, of course, on occasion not to be recognised at all as Philip Larkin suggested when he said*:

They fuck you up, your mum and dad.
> They may not mean to, but they do.
> They fill you with the faults they had
> And add some extra, just for you.
> But they were fucked up in their turn
> By fools in old-style hats and coats,
> Who half the time were soppy-stern
> And half at one another's throats.

* Philip Larkin, 'This Be the Verse', from Collected Poems, Copyright © Estate of Philip Larkin, Reprinted by permission of Faber and Faber, Ltd,

My dad was trained at Imperial College London to be a botanist before he quit to take up the artistic life. When push came to shove, Chelsea Arts College held more sway than cosseting tea plants in Ceylon, as Sri Lanka was then called. And a generous grant from the busy arts philanthropist, Eddie Marsh, saw him on his way to Montmartre for a very traditional grounding in Bohemian life.

For the next 60 years he was mostly involved with painting but was a fine photographer and innovative fabric designer. Mum had a degree in fine arts from Reading University, an amazing achievement for a woman in the 1930's, and became an award-winning botanical illustrator with a string of popular books, published by Collins in the '50s, carrying her illustrations.

They had both chosen the Bohemian life, maybe in response to their upbringing, to which, despite some benefits, they added corrosive poverty to the entrenched emotional disadvantages that I have outlined. Bohemian values and family life don't always go together that well, however attractive they might seem from the outside. I remember hearing John Fowles, the British author of novels with quirky endings, being interviewed on BBC TV in the '70s. He said that artists should not have children because they are too much of a distraction from the work of generating creative output. Perhaps, even being married was not that cool a practice either.

My Dad seemed oblivious to these nuances and he just carried on as a mostly benevolent, sometimes angry and detached bystander while my Mother bore the brunt of all of this, steering the family as best she could with Dad as the occasional player who was more concerned with painting and poodle-faking than paternity and providing.

Dad prided himself on being eccentric, arguing that most eccentric behaviour was doing the obvious whatever the response of people around you might be. However, his definition of eccentricity, did not include taking obvious responsibility for the family finances and the family's emotional well-being. The first pound note was always nailed to the wall and he was the most secretive person in matters of money.

Money problems were the enduring experience of my childhood. As Oscar Wilde said, money is only an issue in life if you haven't got any. I found it shaming and embarrassing to go to school without dinner money because there was none and to have to make do with clothes that were falling apart or too small. Certainly, the intimacy of our family circle, the way we related to each other, was patterned by poverty. When my two shillings and 11 pence dinner money (yes, seven old pennies per day!) disappeared off the mantlepiece clock, it was as if the world had come to an end.

The tribulations delivered by my parents, meant my brother and sister and I were fiercely independent and as self-sufficient as we could be as we each battled to deal with the welfare issues in our own way. Sister

Sally and I chose financial security as a necessary underpinning for our adult lives though we never saw it as an end in itself. Brother Dan was more romantic in his endeavours as a natural history film-maker but always measured his life, apart from its familial aspects, on its creativity. It is clear that our experiences of family life with our parents were the decisive factors in patterning our future relationships.

Despite the lack of money, being raised in a Bohemian household had its benefits. I always saw the world as my oyster and one in which I was free to go anywhere and do anything. My self-esteem was always high as I ploughed a unique furrow unencumbered by matters of class or social mores. I was also an avid learner. Bernie my best friend from Cheshunt Grammar School came from a Jewish working class background and I revelled in trips to his home in Waltham Cross to see how his family lived – and to enjoy the TV teas with baked beans, chips, eggs and bacon served up by his mum Ruby who then disappeared to the tiny kitchen to have her tea on her own. Bernie had a reciprocal experience when visiting us where conversation not food ruled the roost – and his time in our house might coincide with the regular visits by artists and writers like Antonia White, Henry Moore, or Michael Wickham.

The formative influence on my life of my much-troubled father should not, therefore, be under-estimated. He was passionate about the visual arts and literature, music and ideas and enjoyed 'critical' conversations. But he was also broadly disinterested in our lives as children, expecting us to battle on resourcefully, whatever the odds, with little input from him and totally dependent on our mum.

Despite the corrosive nature of his self-centred view of the world, his secretiveness and somewhat ruthless pursuit of his own ends, he was ultimately a creatively gifted human being who dramatically failed to fulfil his potential. His close friend and Jungian psychiatrist, Gerhard Adler, was of the view that Frank had a failure complex; like Midas in reverse – everything valuable he touched turned to dust.

My birthday poem for him follows:

On His Sixty Eighth Birthday

Intolerant and foolish
Generous and wise
Selfish, but not conceited,
Concerned with other lives
No virtue has he
But is partnered by vice
Yet in this conjunction
One man is seen twice
One part is the sea
One part is the land
Only opposites in character
Make the whole man.

In a far off place,
A well-known tyger cries
'Sui generis . . .. Sui generis'
And will not die.

DULWICH, 1 SEPTEMBER 1969

THE WORLD AT LARGE

I left Pinewood in 1949 and was a teenager in the mid
'50s. This was a time when world and country lead-
ers were ancient mainly white males (like Adenauer,
de Gaulle, Churchill, Mao, Menzies, Eisenhower and
Khrushchev) and older male voters ruled the roost. The
pre-eminence of older males seemed to be forever but
then 43-year-old JFK became President of the USA in
1961 when I was 17 and a new era was on us. It was now
politically OK to be under 50.

His spell in power was short-lived. Those of us
around at that time will always remember the moment
we learned the sad news of his assassination. It is strange
how deeply in our memories monumental events like
this are etched. Just as JFK's death was told to me on
the fifth floor of the Waynflete Building at Magdalen
College by David Harland (later Professor of Law at
Sydney Uni), I remember exactly where I was when
9/11 happened (in the TV room in our Australian
family home in Richmond Avenue, Cremorne), and
at a Leichhardt lunch hosted by Richard and Annie
Goodwin when in August 1997 Princess Diana met
her death at the hands of the paparazzi. As the movie

American Graffiti asked – 'where were you in 'sixty two?'

These catastrophic events (we can add the collapse of the Soviet empire in 1989; the demolition of the Berlin Wall; COVID and the global pandemic of 2020 and, as I write, the impact of frightening geo-politics in the Middle East and the Ukraine; not to forget that Artificial Intelligence looks set to destroy traditional democratic processes and principles)) are often harbingers of great change. The assassination of JFK was such an event. The narrow-minded '50s gave way to the open-minded '60s with shock waves of the new reverberating through western society and presenting the idea that anything could happen. My teenage years straddled 1960 and finished just before the '60s were to explode into action with The Beatles in 1964.

Robert Hughes' art book *The Shock of the New* pioneered how artists in the '60s hit the same spot in terms of the impact of modernism on the history of art. All the balls were in the air. Not only could anything happen, but it also felt like you could do anything with your life and bugger the third mortgage.

Traditional social relationships were questioned – especially the role of monogamy and fidelity, the purpose of marriage and the true responsibility for child-rearing. The legalisation of the Pill for all UK women in 1967 transformed contraception practice and gave sexual freedom a new connotation even if there is little doubt that the sexual liberation was still firmly empowering men.

These sharp shifts in the society and culture of western democracies were perplexing for those living through them. Ian McEwen's wonderful book, *On Chesil Beach,* brilliantly captures the social sea-changes that were all happening so quickly and at once that we struggled to find a foothold and stability. I prize this book as it was such an accurate a description of the battered culture of that time.

As an office bearer of the UK YCND (Youth Campaign for Nuclear Disarmament) in the early '60s, I remember so clearly the feeling that it was up to us to create the revolution. And I will always remember the 1963 Aldermaston March when we broke ranks with a group called *Spies for Peace* to shine the spotlight on the Regional Seat of Govt 6 (RSG 6) near Reading as a sign of how government bureaucracies under the banner of Civil Defence were seeking a self-serving bolt hole in case of a nuclear war. This concern was somewhat alleviated for me when we entered Trafalgar Square on that Easter Monday and a London Bobby on duty winked at me as he flipped his lapel badge to reveal his CND badge hidden underneath.

The Female Eunuch was published during this sea-change. In addition, it freed up men to re-evaluate their roles – not just as family members but in the workplace and society at large.

In 1972 Granada decided we should move our offices to an airfield in Park Street, a suburb of St Albans in the Hertfordshire countryside. McGraw Hill, just before I joined them, had made a similar move from Mayfair to Maidenhead. In publishing this was an era of aggregation with the big publishers getting bigger and then rationalising their underlying overheads by moving out of London to cheaper neighbourhoods. The transformational impact was severe because creative media types like commissioning editors and publicists need to be in the thick of it in a way the suburbs cannot deliver. In Park Street the diversity of Soho or Mayfair was traded for lunch in the local pub and 'in house' love relationships between staff members. This dynamic change created much unhappiness and ultimately those affected changed ship as best they could so as to return to city life.

In late 1973, in an entrepreneurial moment, I took the initiative to put on a show of Dad's paintings at the Upper Street Gallery in Islington. One of the visitors to the show was a work colleague of mine, Gill, who I had fallen headlong in love with soon after she had joined Granada Publishing that July.

My relationship with Gill was a product of this dynamic with our isolation in the country strengthening the relationship we had developed.

Despite her innate strength, persistence and courage, Mum occasionally complained. At the Christmas after the Islington show, she reached (not for the first time) the end of her tether. Sitting on my bed crying vociferously, she told me she had hit the wall with Dad and that she was going to leave him.

His affairs were the hidden text for her unhappiness but this event was a matter of extremely bad timing from my point of view. My marriage to dear Liz was in crisis and about to collapse under the urgent weight of my love affair with Gill.

I consoled my mother, telling her not to be so stupid. After all, she'd been married for over 40 years and couldn't possibly contemplate building a new life on her own at the ripe old age of 60. She stayed. I didn't. A week or so later, Gill and I were sleeping on the floor of friends' flat in Highbury as we pushed out the boat on our relationship and closed those of our now previous marriages.

My mother did not let on about the juxtaposition of her crisis with mine but she did remark in tears that I was the only businessman in the family; Bohemian values at work where commerce is seen to be a corruption of the soul. She hardly understood that my financial success as a publisher was a statement in direct opposition to the moneyless Bohemian culture, and which might also explain why I failed 'O' Level Art!

In retrospect, I am puzzled as to the origin of any ideas which suggest you may go out of your way to exploit a situation for your own advantage. I believe as we grow up that we may, from time to time, flirt with dangerous behaviours that are very close to crossing the line from spirited and acceptable play to dangerous abuse. I can certainly recall a couple of moments which I have never been happy about when my volatile temper took me to that brink, first with Liz and later with Gill. But civility has won out, I hope, on balance.

Fortunately, these activities were isolated and did not lead to a lifelong involvement with similar pursuits. In Cheshunt, and, then, when we moved to the village of Lasham in Hampshire, I spent most of my spare time playing football and cricket, reading, and, after pubs became available, drinking Watneys Brown Ale and Worthington E. I goofed around on my push-bike usually with my kid brother Dan who, incidentally, seemed to me to have more success in attracting girls than I did although he asserted later on that the only difference between us in affairs of the heart was that I married all my girl friends!

Dan who spent two years at boarding school when we lived in Cheshunt, just 17 months my junior, was an ever-present part of my teenage years in Hampshire. We played football and cricket for the same school and then adult teams like Alton Town and the Trojan Wanderers (a habit that lasted until I left for Australia in 1983). We were very close, His period at Hadham Hall, an agricultural boarding school in Hertfordshire, when I just 13, created a big gap in my daily life but, fortunately, did not last for very long.

—

Back in 1960, I was deeply perplexed at just how you go about asking a girl for a date. And the fear of rejection was nearly always enough to block experimentation. It is not surprising that my first date was organised for me by Sally, a classmate, acting as a go-between, with a girl two-years my junior, about whom I had obsessed about for weeks. I was 17 or so. We arrived at the rendezvous—the local Odeon cinema – in Farnham, Surrey and in we went. I can't remember the movie but it might as well have been *Puberty Blues*.

I spent the whole evening anguishing about putting an arm around her and noticing a boy in front of me who, as I put it in a poem a little later on, had no such scruples as he attended to his date 'with predilection, at inspection of the bony bit between the neck and pit of the arm, wool covered, well-loved with charm'. Lesley and I exchanged hardly a word and after it had finished, she rushed off to catch her bus home to Grayshott. We never went out or even talked again. My obsession, this time, was vanquished.

This experience told me how pathetic I was and how impossible it seemed to me to start a relationship. It was all to do with the fear of being rejected which I felt so strongly that I thought it was better not to make a pass. Apart from Linda, there were Jenny, Clare and Annabelle – all fanciable and equally unapproachable. Nevertheless, the 'she loves me, she loves me not' conundrum is more than the process of removing the petals on a flower. It is, in fact, a great big safety net to ensure we go through the appropriate considerations before jumping into the void. And the irony is when you do step off the cliff, the outcome is sort of obvious. For every relationship I have ever eventually been in, she was always going to say 'yes' even if it did take a day or two to eventuate! You didn't need to consider strategy or read self-help books or seek the advice of friends. It was always going to be.

The most extreme version of this came with the events preceding my third marriage (now in its fourth delightful decade) when Susie called me in Double Bay from her St Ives home to arrange a meeting between us at *The Oaks* in Sydney's Neutral Bay. I responded and half an hour later, in the Military Road bar, she explained she wanted a cooling off period before we committed to taking the relationship further. We'd been dating for four months which included a splendid overlap in our respective vacations to Europe when she met my four children for the first time.

This was a highly emotional period in my life. I was in Australia to start up a law and business publishing imprint for Longman Group publishers having left the UK and my three older children for 'maybe three-years. But not more'. Within four months of arrival in Sydney, Gill and I split up. Personal migration, relationship changing, business novation . . . these are each the drivers of mental stress and anxiety let alone with their impact when taken together.

Despite being ready for therapy, back at *The Oaks* three gin and tonics later, having been in deep and serious agreement about her concerns, I asked her very

quietly 'Susie, would you like to move in with me?'
'Oh, all right then', she said and three weeks later we
were partners in crime at the Sydney Harbour end of
Raglan Street in Mosman, in a sandstone folly from
1914, called *The Castle*- complete with Sydney Harbour,
Taronga Zoo, fishing, funnel web spiders and termites.

So rehearsed and planned relationship moves seem
unnecessary in retrospect. My first girl-friend is another
case in point. Liz lived in Shalden – the next village to
me – and was part of a large classy family with a very
active social life. As newcomers to the Hampshire countryside, we were delighted to contact them and their
network of teenage friends. This involved going to posh
ballroom dances but also pubs and clubs in the area.
And drinking at Liz's parents' pretty Georgian country
house, lots of Gordon's gin mixed with Dubonnet or
Vermouth ; Scotch and wine – easily trumping my parents' line of ten-bob Cyprus Sherry and the undrink-
able cloudy tepid home-made beer made in demi-john
by my Dad.

For the first months, Liz and I were part of a crowd.
I liked her a lot especially in her eccentric, arty sort of
way but, once again, it was an outsider – my brother-
in-law – who suggested as we did the washing up in
our Lasham farmhouse that I should ask Liz out on
a date. This was a proposal I might not have reached
on my own. But Liz said 'yes' and we set off down a
path which would deliver in due course three delightful
children over a 12-year relationship.

When we set sail, my spirit and commitment were naturally monogamous. Not for religious or other moral reasons but because I really believed (and still do) in the idea of romantic love. William Shakespeare and John Keats, were my muses. The idea of 'sleeping around' was foreign to me. I was also well aware that the idea of playing the field was not viewed equally for boys and girls. Our culture has been deeply inequitable on this topic being ready to applaud the boys (sowing their oats) and censure the girls (slut/whore/tart) for exactly the same behaviours. This single asymmetry is the key foundation of gender inequality in the West and gender abuse in the East. And all the other horrors in between.

'Going steady' was my preferred way of relating so when, after we'd been dating for about two years, Liz teamed up with an art-school colleague it was as if my world had fallen apart. I had never experienced jealousy before and I was very surprised at the depth of my severely jangled feelings.

Intellectually I had always argued, somewhat pompously, that jealousy was the expression of a property right in the relationship with the unloving one and that it was to be frowned on as a matter of course. But one of the major learnings I made, the would-be adult, is that our intellectual and emotional selves are so different – to the extent they lead us to wildly different points of view, among which the emotional is much more basic than the intellectual. You may intellectualise the rationale of what is happening when your girl goes off with someone else, but the emotional truth is something quite different.

Even though we were no longer going out together, Liz and I went on a camping holiday that we were already committed to, in the Dordogne in France, with my brother, Dan, and friends Bernie, Julian and Jenny (who had been selected by Liz's parents as a chaperone). This was a challenge and I would say one that I totally failed. I behaved badly towards Liz with my anger always just a millimetre away. I just couldn't accept that we had split up. And sharing such a small space for five rain-sodden weeks made the whole process a nightmare for me and pretty uncomfortable for Liz.

The only upside was that I was only a few weeks away from going up to Oxford and that prospect kept me looking to the future with a different kind of anxiety from that in the holiday tent. The holiday was also negative in that our prime mission included visiting the Lascaux caves near Montignac with their famous prehistoric cave paintings. It was August 1963. Alas the caves had been closed forever just a month before we arrived because natural light was fading the paintings and the repro version wouldn't open until 1983.

I survived the holiday and, subsequently, never discussed Liz's response to it. The irony is that when I got to Magdalen College, Oxford it took me a week or two to date a new girl, who was training at the Ox & Cow Secretarial College and knocked around with a group of late teenagers that I had joined as we experimented in our new environment. I dropped Liz a kind note to let her know that I was OK and she needn't worry about me anymore. But she did. Her reply was immediate and she asked me to meet her at Oxford Station that Saturday morning on the London Express train – fondly known locally as the 'Fornication Flyer'.

This I did and by mid-day, I was in the arms of a surprising reconciliation, joined at the hip once more with a very insistent girl. We were now firmly re-entrenched, with Liz coming to Oxford when she could and our spending vacation time in Hampshire with family and friends. We were very happy.

The social milieu of this time has, as already said, been brilliant captured by Ian McEwen in *On Chesil Beach* which brought tears to my eyes almost fifty years later, prompting me to send Liz a copy from Australia to Wales for her to share these special memories with me. We did not share the problem (premature ejaculation) of the couple in McEwen's book – in fact the opposite! – but we did share the social milieu so painfully described in the book. This was a world that frowned on sex before marriage and in which the expectations of middle-class kids were firmly controlled by parents and private schools.

Our sexual relationship was also taking place in a world before the Pill was readily available. We used luck, condoms, withdrawal and the Catholic methods for contraception. Liz and I had a code. The 'Knorr

Mushroom Soup' code. Each month after Liz had a period she'd give me, without a word, a packet of Knorr Mushroom Soup as a sign.

Then, in July 1964, there was no soup. Nor was there Knorr soup in August.

The no-Knorr-soup pregnancy was with us. I had finished my first year at Oxford and Liz was finishing her time at a 'finishing' school, Pax Hill, in the house once-owned by Lord Baden-Powell the founder of the Scout movement, in the village of Bentley – later to be immortalised (for some) as *The Village* on TV – a village my parents were to move to in a year or so.

Her finishing process now came to a full stop and the two families involved held a 'what do we do now?' meeting. Liz's parents wanted her to have an abortion – a moderately surprising idea since it was broadly illegal in those days and, anyway, they were the stalwarts of the local church. My parents were more open-minded saying it was up to Liz and me. We had no doubt that we wanted to go ahead with the pregnancy and Tom, in all his glory, was born on the first day of spring 1965, an indomitable and undeniable human spirit and, now, a professor of psychology at the University of Wales in Cardiff.

Liz and I were very young to engage in family life and I have to admit from my point of view although I was committed to Liz, our lack of worldly experience might prove problematic later on. Relationships are full of hidden truths which we deny only for them to emerge fairly consistently.

This dilemma is partnered by another; the need for the protagonist in a split to rewrite the narrative of a relationship so as to justify leaving. This is almost always a cheap trick and reflects badly on the protagonist – a trick I have never consciously employed although I am a very self-centred being. I am lucid about my love for Liz which was grounded in a shared adolescence, a shared loss of virginity, deep friendship and surprising parenthood but was, from my angle, unlikely to withstand the steps of time. And this is one of many reasons why we operate better now, despite the pain and, admittedly from my point of view, as an extended family.

There is an interesting side issue to what I have just said. A close friend confided in me her mistrust of relationships where there is a commitment to be truthful at all times and to be forever open as to the way you feel. She confessed that there were clear no-go areas in her marriage that she felt wise to steer clear of as they progressed.

The '60s were particularly difficult for couples as the idea of sexual freedom and 'open' marriage took hold. In his novel *Couples* John Updike brilliantly tracked one version of this but the destructiveness of much of this is a topic for the next chapter.

BREAKING RANKS

So, there we were in 1965. Young parents with our lives still to come, willingly wed but for me with a hint of reservation. Our future was no longer what it might have been.

The upshot of this was a vulnerability that was to become exposed after just two years. As a species, I always think of us humans as being intellectually advanced and emotionally retarded. This is nowhere truer than in the way we relate to each other, as friends and lovers. Emotional dilemmas become entanglements that bind us so strongly that we don't know what to do even if our brain has some good suggestions for our consideration.

Occasionally, the brain has the final – or at least – a powerful say. When I was at Essex University, in 1966, doing an MA in the Sociology of Literature, I fell head over heels in love with Julia in a way I had never thought possible. I was obsessed. Every waking moment was focused on her, with the next meeting the most important event in my life. My tutor was the eminent philosopher Alasdair MacIntyre. One evening we were in the campus bar and I asked what action would he take if he were married with a child like me but in love with someone else. He said that in life you will occasionally encounter problems which seem to have no willing resolution and that what I had described sounded very much like one of them.

'There is only one course of action I would

recommend with your problem,' he confided, 'and that is to wait until it is no longer a problem.' The wise nuances of his advice still ring true today. Stepping back from the role of the protagonist and simply waiting for the situation to evolve organically has much to recommend it.

My relationship with Julia continued, nevertheless, but the idea of leaving Liz for her was firmly set aside. Our marriage had strengthened with the births of Sam and Tabitha in the following four years as if some kind of settling in was at hand. Three children under the age of seven and a publishing career on the burst, taken together, are enough to stress even the strongest relationships. But when Gill came on to the scene in 1973, the reality of my affair with Julia came into focus, once more, with the return of the pressure to forsake Liz for fresh fields. I didn't have an Alasdair MacIntyre to steady my ship and the pressure to leave, this time, was becoming undeniable.

I did, however, try to contextualise what was going on with Gill by asking myself – is this relationship simply a substitute for the fact that I had never been a bachelor male testing the free market or 'playing the field'? Were the sentiments of 'being in love' an illusion and rationalisation for the thrill of the chase and making up for missed opportunities? I didn't think so but how could I be sure? I decided to test it by taking the unusual initiative of womanising, of sleeping around. This did not come naturally to me but if all my problems were a lack of sexual experience (only three lovers as I approached 30) then maybe I should give it a go. Consequently, I had a fling with Anna (another work colleague) for whom I had no deep feelings other than finding her physically attractive. The liaison had zero impact on my understanding of where I was with Gill and my response, if any, was to feel badly about using Anna to test some rather poor hypotheses.

My focus on Gill deepened. I felt I had to be with her. This moment brought with it an equally undeniable sense of confusion. Like a lot of pathetic males, I have always liked to be liked and the opprobrium which I knew would be vented on me by some of my friends and family was hard to take on board. A close family member later said to Julia at a drinks party, when Julia asked how I was going with Gill, 'Oh we never talk about *him*'.

There was, of course, some basis for the opprobrium I encountered because I have to accept that despite my marriage to Liz at 20, and becoming the father to three gorgeous kids, my behaviour in my twenties showed a fair amount of disloyalty and lack of commitment. I was behaving in a way my Dad would have recognised in that I was distancing myself from my children as I pursued selfish interests. I had in fact been playing the field for almost ten years in a selfish way, while kidding myself it was otherwise.

Every moment I spend looking back on that period in my love life brings with it a deep sense of remorse and wishing it could have been otherwise for the five of us involved in my first family. Of course, those feelings are now counterbalanced by the children produced by Gill and Susie who are equally undeniable.

This chapter in my life about growing up had now come to an end with my second marriage opening up in front of me. If I had learned anything about the process it is that the idea of sleeping around has a strong affinity with market economics and that, on balance, economics is a very poor tool not only for measuring social progress but also for measuring the effectiveness of relationships.

The irony in the process is that it is ultimately all about you and not the people you are relating to. However I got there, my broken marriage felt like I was breaking ranks leaving behind a litany of family relationships and friendships which would never be the same.

Playlist

Danny Kaye, The Ugly Duckling
Patti Page, How Much is that Doggie in the Window
Peggy Lee, Fever
Marilyn Monroe, Diamonds Are a Girl's Best Friend
Paul Simon, Me and Julie Down by the School Yard
St Etienne, Only Love Can Break Your Heart
Cliff Richard & The Shadows, Move It
Unit 4 + 2, Concrete and Clay

The Beatles, Strawberry Fields
Bert Kaempfert, A Swinging Safari
Beethoven, The Kreutzer Sonata
Sydney Torch, The Archer's Theme
Buddy Holly, Peggy Sue
Louis Prime, Yes We Have No Bananas
Madness, Our House
Neil Young, The Field of Opportunity
The Beatles, Let it Be
The Teddy Bears, To Know Him is to Love Him
Muriel Anderson, Lady Pamela
Sister Sledge, We Are Family
Danny Kaye, Tubby the Tuba
Queen, Bohemian Rhapsody
Leonard Cohen, Chelsea Hotel
Burl Ives, Venezuela
The Beatles, Revolution
Led Zeppelin, Stairway to Heaven
The McGuire Sisters, Love and Marriage
Elton John, Daniel
Dave Brubeck, Take Five
The Righteous Brothers, You've Lost That Loving Feeling
Ray Charles, Let the Good Times Roll
The Zombies, She's Not There
Sonny, & Cher, I Got You Babe
Barry McGuire, Eve of Destruction
P P Arnold, The First Cut is the Deepest
The Drifters, There Goes My Baby
Joan Baez, Diamonds and Rust

3

SEX FOR LOVE AND
LOVE FOR SEX

The Economics of Love

Busy old fool unruly Donne
Love is not a bleak zero sum –
A finite natural resource
To be share-traded on the Bourse.
That swan of Avon, William S,
Captured its warmth with great success
Juliet knows the more she gives
The more love she has that lives and lives.
Not for her Eliot's wasted land
Where making love's a deadly hand
Not just some record on the gramophone
Romeo's voice is love's real tone.
Love would make Isaac Newton blush
Defy his laws, an apple crushed,

Fred Hoyle knew matter can be created
Its continual emergence never sated.
Welcome to the love economy,
A world of other-autonomy.
A place devoid of hates and fears,
The place I'm in when you are near.
Love is vicinity.
Love is divinity.
Love is infinity.
The economics of love.

ROZELLE, 2016

As a teenager, I was intrigued by the idealistic collision on matters of love and sex between the great poets of my grammar school education – Donne, Marvel, Shakespeare, Eliot, Keats and Wordsworth. There is, of course, no substitute for real life (an attitude rejected by much pornography to everyone's disadvantage), but tracking attitudes through poetry is a rewarding process because of poetry's immediate contact with both our emotions and our intellect. Love and sex are as inextricably involved with form and content as the words of a Shakespearean sonnet or a Donne eulogy.

In my corner, I found Shakespeare and Keats embracing love and sex as an inextricably connected duality and in the opposite corner, the 'blue' corner perhaps, was Eliot with his catholic distaste of sex and almost neurotic fear of love. Donne is shoulder to shoulder with TS and shared his negativity by seeing love as a finite commodity not to be given up readily.

Wordsworth is tricky. The Lucy poems capture fabulously the mortality of love but are written by a man obsessed by Lucy as an object. His objectification of femininity in the form of a pubescent and vulnerable working-class country girl is ultimately a bit of a worry because once such objectification becomes filled with any sexual meaning then the path to paedophilia opens up before you. John Donne placed his women in a similar plight by 'canonising' their existence, thus removing them from tactile reality. I'll return to this topic in the next chapter on passion and romantic love.

Australian journalist Elizabeth Farrelly touched on the topic of this chapter in 2017 in an article in *The Sydney Morning Herald*. She said 'Hardwired or not, male and female sex drives are, by and large, different. Men are driven to spread the seed; women to nest. This is neither universal nor exhaustive, but it generates the truism that men want love for sex and women want sex for love.'* I also reflect that once sex and love are separated into different pursuits all sorts of problems arise. One of my closest publishing friends was a notorious womaniser who reckoned that the next pass he would make was a matter of duty. No wonder his nickname was the 'Groper'. Standing at the traffic

---

* https://www.smh,com,au/opinion/
  is-chivalry-dead-in-this-sexted-up-world-20171229-h0b5g1,html

lights in Taylor Square on one of his many visits to Sydney, he confided in me 'you know, Oli, I have never been in love with anybody'. Sex was a barrier to love for him, as he focused on his sexual prowess (I later gathered he was good at it) and rejected the human commitment that is the badge of love (which he never offered).

Propositions like Farrelly's are always up for the testing but after a lifetime of close encounters with womankind, I'd say it is spot on. The answer lies in the genes, for sure.

The proposition, also, reflects the crux of this book on which I would now like to expand around what, playfully, I call the seven relationship spins. These are the attributes on which, in any order, seem to me to be the virtues that successful love *and* sex relationships are built. In any order they are; kindness; honesty; trust; values; commitment; respect and collaboration.

Readers should note that these qualities are not mutually exclusive. My life, may be like yours, has been a systemic hotch-potch with all these attributes bumping into each other to create unexpected outcomes. And no one will get an A grade report card for all of them.

KINDNESS

In a graduate address in 2013, Professor of English and Booker prize-winning novelist George Saunders was outlining to the convocation class at Syracuse University his regrets. Forty years after an incident at his school, he identified lack of kindness as being his major regret.[*]

He says 'Because kindness, it turns out, is *hard* – it starts out all rainbows and puppy dogs, and expands to include . . . well, *everything*.'

For Liz

I regret the way I changed your life
When you were powerless to intervene,
Rudely reshaping your expectations
And what it would mean for you to have been.

I rejoice the way our children have grown
When we were powerless to intervene
Beautifully shaping their destinies
On a stage that is now their scene.

Regret, rejoice – it's a choice
We don't have power to call
Bless you now and forever, Liz
(I lean against the wall).

ROZELLE 2017

My poem *For Liz* is addressed to my first wife and summarises the debt I owe her and offers my reflection

---

[*] https://6thfloor,blogs,nytimes,com/2013/07/31/
george-saunderss-advice-to-graduates

on our marriage break-up 50 years ago. Henry James endorsed the importance of kindness when he said: 'Three things in human life are important. The first is to be kind. The second is to be kind. And the third is to be kind.'*

This feels right as another rendering of Kant's Golden Rule (treat others as you'd like them to treat you) and yet if there is one general illumination of love relationships in today's world it is the conspicuous lack of kindness so often in play. Stressed couples have the amazing capacity to descend below the normal bickering that we all are prone to, to treat each other unkindly, as unspoken enemies. However, these declarations of war are rarely explicit so negotiating a ceasefire becomes problematic. And, on occasion, it is only the outsiders that are aware of the awfulness of it all and are frustrated at the lack of action within. We all have friends who have gone through the transformation of a break up in the ghastliest circumstances. Do they look back on these experiences as be normal or deviant?

When I look back on my leaving Liz, with three children under the age of 10, because of the damage it caused, I myself ask 'How could I have done that?' I also ask 'was the separation really as inevitable as it felt at the time?'

---

* Overheard by his nephew, Billy James, in 1902; quoted in Leon Edel, Henry James: A Life, vol V: The Master 1901-1916 (Rupert Hart Davis, 1972),

Ironically, Liz is one of the kindest people I have met as her disposition in the last half century proves. And Susie is without equal on this score. They have both been role models for me.

As J K Rowling offered in *Harry Potter*: 'Indifference and neglect often do much more damage than outright dislike.'** And it is indifference and neglect that drives failures of kindness as much as any other characteristics.

—

Kindness is not just a virtue to pattern our personal lives, it is also needed in business life, in the life of organisations whatever their purpose. It often gets excluded on the basis that 'business is business' and validates unkind behaviour in the interest of share-holders and similar financial. As a publisher for over 50 years, I have lived through unkind decisions affecting authors as well as staff members – and on one or two occasions affecting me. I worked for a difficult boss, Alewyn Birch, at Granada Publishing in the UK, who decided to reduce my responsibilities (I was a keen divisional publisher) by taking one of my lists and offering it to a new publisher he wanted to hire but who needed to do more. Despite the fact I had turned around the

** Dumbledore to Harry talking about Sirius's treatment of Kreacher, (Harry Potter & the Order of the Phoenix Bloomsbury, London 2007, p, 834)

performance of the sailing book list over the previous two years. I was suddenly out in the cold. I resigned, informing Alewyn that I wasn't in the market for less responsibility at the tender age of 32.

I tried to be fair with my staff as my role as a boss increased but I was not immune from being unkind. I retrenched my legal retail bookshop manager in Sydney when I owned the business, responding to pressure from her manager who demanded the change. I regretted what had happened and this was emphasised by the resignation six-months later of the manager I had supported. I should have resisted what I had been asked to do.

Kindness is a tricky topic because we tend to see it as being an innate characteristic rather than a learned disposition. A kind person is not the same as a person acting kindly. There is a strong link between kindness and vulnerability in that when I act kindly I am opening myself to responses that may bring my integrity into question. Was the act a trade? Is there a hidden meaning about me the giver rather than you the receiver of my felicitations? Kindness can, thus, be seen as a weakness but at the same time it demands a lot of courage, especially in situations where social pressures are asking us to respond unkindly to the acts of others.

There is a second web of vulnerability that links to kindness. The kind person is usually tolerant without so rigid a set of moral principles as to condemn to the flames those who lack their convictions. They are by nature open to persuasion and to assess each situation on its merits. Outsiders may see this attribute as some kind of failure but the bottom line is that there isn't a bottom line – just an invitation to treat people with respect and honour wherever they have landed. And above all to listen and not pontificate.

The fierce passionate animosity and anger that often attends relationship breakdown precludes kindness. But not forever. Although for each of us the experience is unique, we can see around us that there are many pathways to the future. In my experience it takes two years or so to recover from the initial train-wreck of separation. This should not be seen as a resolution as sometimes there can be no resolution. The grief that accompanies separation, rather like death, may last for ever. Nevertheless. the pathways that we may follow may suggest we can choose how we react, sometimes in spite of ourselves, but we do have the capacity to act otherwise.

The jurisprudence of our lives in western democracies is based on the notion of free will, that we can choose what we do. However, damaged we may be because of our genetic make-up; the hand dealt for us by our parents, the travails of childhood, and the impact of society on our lives, we are in every way responsible for who we are and what we do.

The need for kindness is linked to circumstances. However fractured relationships may be, formative events will take place that require kindness from the protagonists as a way of getting through. Death is probably the most significant of these, closely followed by birth, psychological and psychiatric disorders, poverty, job failure and the like.

As for me, I think I have got part of the way there on the kindness spectrum. My Achilles heel is a lack of sensitivity to the needs of others which springs from my self-centredness, offset, I hope, by my generosity and responsiveness when the situation demands.

HONESTY

The virtues driving a good life are, as we are beginning to see, as tricky as can be. Honesty, in the sense of openness, of fessing up to your involvement in a situation, can lead us into difficult situations where what we want to be honest about may be hurtful to our partners. My friend's reticence, mentioned earlier, at making all subjects explicit on the relationship agenda expresses this point. There are 'no-go' areas in every relationship which, if entered, may seriously endanger its sustainability. The diplomatic sensibility that this idea embodies is not presented to outlaw openness but to recognise that for each of us our sense of self differs from those of our partners such that an exact contiguity is most unlikely.

The topics for battle tend to be small and best unharvested. In my mildly obsessive-compulsive way, I am a collector. Books, kitsch, green majolica china, clocks and fob watches, sentimental and religious prints (apart from wives and children!) have at various times in my life been the focus of my attention, representing to my third wife, Susie, luggage from my past time – a life she had not shared. Susie, in turn, is a bit of a minimalist and if there has been one continuous irritant it lurks on the clutter to cleanliness continuum. I mean 'one person's collection is another person's clutter'. We have also down-sized from Cremorne to Rozelle which inevitably puts pressure on available space.

I have dealt with this to the extent that it is up to me by avoiding conflict and submitting, I stress voluntarily, as and when needed. For example, almost the last of my sentimental and religious prints were sold at Lawson's in Sydney just a year ago as a container with other examples was on its way to the UK to the homes of my four children living there.

My book collection of around 3500 titles is well under 50% of what it was just five years ago, as is my collection of green Majolica plates. My sister, Sally, remarked to me once, 'nobody needs 100 green plates' an accurate summation, ironically from one of the greatest hoarders I have ever known! Add to that my 500 LPs and 1000 CDs and you get the picture (oh yes and about 60 paintings and prints hanging on the walls).

There is a second honesty feature too. If you are by aptitude a serial monogamist like me, then being honest to yourself is as important as the outward facing kind. A feature of most relationship breakdowns is denial.

When I learned why Gill left me in 1984, I 'honestly' had no idea of the problems that she was dealing with. Top of the list was what I learned it wasn't. It wasn't that she no longer loved me, or just that she was in love with someone else. It was to do with power. Her perception was that she had never had the power in our relationship to do what she wanted to do. That men always made her into some kind of trophy when what she wanted to be was herself.

But her list was more than this one item. I had betrayed a wife's trust by fooling around with other women – activities that I did not see as inevitable or essential but ones where my pursuit of pleasure and self-satisfaction had taken precedence. Once Gill was aware of my dalliances, the contract was broken. She wanted absolute loyalty from her partner and I let her down on this core point. My behaviour was dishonest, unacceptable and as it turned out destructive. And, ironically, as it turned out, not in my interest.

The lesson I have drawn from this is quite clear. Relationships in which love *and* sex thrive side by side are almost always unique and committed. One to one. No intruders. You can have successful relationships based just on sex or just on love without that unique quality, but if you want both, the foundation I have learned for deep intimacy, then stay fully focused on the one relationship all the time. Sequential monogamy, if you will!

My final major learning on the honesty stakes is

how difficult it is to rescue situations which you have blessed with a lie. As a teenager at a party in Shalden in Hampshire, UK, where my first in-laws lived, I sneaked off at 10pm to The Golden Pot, pub a couple of miles away, to get some Embassy cigarettes.

In the pub car-park I backed Liz's family white Austin A35 saloon car into a pillar-red post box in the car park, denting the boot. I returned and parked the car in the garage. The next morning, I said nothing about the incident and when asked by Liz whether I had driven the car I said 'no'. Unfortunately, I had reparked the car in a different part of the home garage from where it had been parked before I borrowed it, so clearly it had been driven by somebody.

I then went off to play cricket in the town of Liss, Hampshire, for Alton Town. As we packed up after the game, a police car drove into the cricket ground with two policemen looking for me. It turned out that the bumped boot of the A35 had red paint on it and they guessed it could match a post-box. The pub was on the list of likely venues and the publican told the enquiring bobbies that, yes, Oliver had come into the pub just last night to buy cigarettes.

Although this was no *Midsummer Murders,* I felt deeply ashamed at being found out. I also recognised how the initial lie had led me down a pathway that I would not have normally chosen. Relationships suffer from the same problem. Once you tell a fib e.g. in answer to 'where were you last night?' without disclosing you'd been in the pub chatting up female work colleagues, you are heading for trouble. Relationships can withstand enormous pressures but lying and denial are lethal. Organisations suffer the same problems when being requested to explain disruptive HR behaviours implemented against the interests of the staff. When I worked for Oyez Publishing, the law publishers in the UK, our owners decided to sell the business. We put together a management buyout proposal which involved our raising via house mortgages with our staff, about £2.5 million. This would have been the best result for all of us but, at the end of the day, the owners went for the highest bidder – Pearson Longman. It would be hard to argue they were lying to us but we had expected a decision in favour of the staff.

TRUST

Trust is a highly elusive commodity which is very hard to define and defend and easily lost. I think it thrives on the Golden Rule but that is not enough because there may be ways you'd like to be treated that others would abhor. In a relationship, oral sex maybe something you'd like to receive but your partner would neither want to receive nor give. Thus, the joke that for a woman to stop giving head to her boyfriend, all she needs to do is marry him! The Golden Rule is ultimately self-serving whereas the prime direction in relationships must be in the direction of the 'significant other'.

When you lose trust, as happened to me in both of

my first full-time relationships and triggered, for example, when I slept somewhat gratuitously (like many other attendees in Frankfurt out to have a good time) with a publishing colleague at *The Frankfurt Book Fair*, the way back is very hard. I wanted to put it right but the changed dynamic of the way we interacted made that very difficult to achieve. And Gill was never in a forgiving mood once I had burst the trust bubble. Her response was to look out for revenge in whatever shape or male form it might appear.

The loss of trust is not necessarily terminal. Many relationships survive, running on trust-empty, because the alternatives do not seem attractive or because the logistical infrastructure that has been developed in social, economic and cultural terms is too dense to enable a break-up.

So what is trust? How does it show itself?

First and foremost, trust is when we can rely with confidence on the behaviours, however imperfect, of our partners to present a predictable balance between their needs and our needs so that the needs of the relationship can flourish. These behaviours aren't necessarily the only ones that make sense as, often, trust presents a sense of a working compromise between what's good for me and what's good for my partner but is not usually presented as a trade-off between the two. In its most virtuous emanation it suggests that if I do what is good for you it will be good for me.

Trust is a gentle attribute. It's not like attraction or

lust, obsession or charisma. It's more like the connecting tissue holding each partner in a web of confidence about who we are, in being together and what lies ahead. Its subtlety is, perhaps, best expressed with the idea that you need to be wary of anybody who states 'you can trust me'. Relationship are knee-deep in situations in which it is the assertive claims that are made about the things that are the most questionable. To 'trust me', you might add 'I'd never do something like that. . .'; 'I know what I am like. . .'; 'You are the only person in the world for me'; 'I get on really well with your mum'!

My relationship with Susie is squarely founded on trust. It's always been there, even when we were dealing with the problematic aftermath of my second marriage. And the day to day bickering, that we are really very good at, has never descended to those more than trivial levels that are so often the sign of a trust deficit. The outstanding difference Susie has made for me has been her unwavering argument from day one (given my CV) about the importance of fidelity and trust in the development of intimacy in our relationship. Organisations need trust too. None more so than those operating in environments which are highly uncertain for participants. In my time publishing has had to withstand the slings and arrows of outrageous digitisation. Not to mention the unstoppable impact of conglomeration on an industry that often excels as a cottage industry rather than a 'big business'. Trust is a major source of certainty in these uncertain situations.

One cute measure of your trust-health is whether your conversations with your partner are conducted in the first person or second person singular. The use of the first person is very healthy. It asserts your views and needs without admonishment. For example, 'I'd like you to spend less money on eating out because it will help our budget' is a far stronger statement than 'You are always spending money on eating out and we can't afford it'. The 'you always do this, you always do that' dynamic is a recipe for confrontation. I am super sensitive to it. Whereas 'I would like you to this, I would like you to do that' is a recipe for negotiation. Trust thrives in the latter condition but heads for the hills in the former.

Ironically, the reverse is relevant for organisations where we want our partners to address problems in the first person and not the third.

VALUES

Values, what I like to call 'worldviews', are the unwritten life-force of a successful relationship. They represent the values which drive us and define our purpose over and above the day-to-day imperatives suggested by, among other things, our need for survival. Families in survival mode, like my family of origin until an elderly aunt died and left us some money, often find the values game a bit of an indulgence but we were, nevertheless, a 'values-full' family and possibly too much so in the way Bohemian people like to live. Success is even more assured when the values shared are implicit in the way we behave with each other and don't need negotiating step by step.

This sounds simple but, like most of the things under discussion, it is not. We don't go through a values-audit as part of the process of getting together but we can become very sensitive to them when things are falling apart. Simple truths are hard fought to put into practice and lie at the other side of the complexities of building a relationship. We spend a lot of time getting it wrong and the values-jungle offers a tangle of undergrowth to be cut through if we are to move towards a deeper harmony. Liz and I shared a strong value-set in the 'sixties only for its power to become sidelined by my change of focus. Now, fifty years on, I can see more clearly how my behaviour side-lined important links between us but did not destroy them.

There is a strong link between values and trust. The balance required in trusting each other expresses itself here as well. Values by their nature are pointing outwards to the world in which our worldviews are directed. It is rewarding to share the same values but at the same time we need to preserve our sense of self – particularly when one partner is the value-driver and assumes that the other will fall in line. Some values-based relationships can survive with little else keeping the couple together. We often talk about a marriage of convenience where love is not the sticky agent binding the two together. Shared values, for example in arranged marriages, would seem to be a priority for their relationships to succeed. The reverse is usually fatal. When all there is is love and the value sets are miles apart, the heat will eventually cool and you are left pulling in different directions and never the twain shall meet.

The best relationship values-sets are likely to be ones that overlap. Where there is enough common ground to hold you both together but enough difference to support your sense of self and to provide a source of learning for your partner. This has been particularly true for my relationship with Susie which has thrived on the balance so described.

On the publishing front, I have experienced situations where crises which threaten to unseat the rider are salvaged by values and trust. The most significant moment was when I was running IBC Australia for my UK partners with a minor shareholding and major responsibility. We went from a standing start in 1987 with three significant takeovers to a grinding halt two years later when the rapidity of our growth and my over optimistic outlook meant we had to make changes.

The initial move was to bring in a new CEO and move me to be non-executive Chairman – in effect an impolite sacking from my founding role. These changes were prepared without my knowledge, a fait accompli which stopped me in my tracks. My UK boss came out to Sydney to push through the changes but I decided not to play ball and gave him a simple option. Either retain my role as Executive Chairman with a general manager reporting to me or sack me with a suitable payout.

He chose the former; he was in line with my values as to what was appropriate and I trusted him to back me up. And in 1990 I completed a management buy-out of the IBC business and, at last, had my own business in play, a business that I owned 100%

ATTRACTION

Fractures

You shattered me with your brown eye
And came amid the pieces with levelled hand
Making from my pieces your own jigsaw
In the slow-turning of the once rock sand

BATTERSEA, 1967

When I first compiled the list of the key attributes that for me create a successful relationship, the question of physical attraction did not appear on it. Silly me. Why? Because physical attraction is the bedrock (pun intended!) on which a relationship is built. It's an intriguing topic and one which creates a minefield out of the possibilities that confront you as you progress.

The physical responses that you have to a potential partner are the most important first steps in a relationship – particularly if you are male. It is estimated that men consider the love-making potential of everyone they meet and actively think about sex every twelve waking minutes. This filter is extremely powerful and sets up an immediate rejection of many people that are being met.

Philosophically this sexual-rejection lever is very superficial despite Oscar Wilde's letting us off the hook when he says in *A Picture of Dorian Grey* that 'It is only shallow people who do not judge by appearances. The true mystery of the world is the visible, not the invisible'.

I have no doubt that people can become beautiful in your eyes as you get to know them better. Appreciation of people's attractiveness changes overtime – in both directions, up and down. And it is one of the themes of this book that the concomitants that make up attraction are aggregated over time and operate way beyond the drive for sex. This is the basis for healthy intimacy in a relationship.

The bind that these comments create is this. You need attraction to get started but there is no guarantee that it will deliver. In my own life I have been attracted to people not just sexually but as friends who just aren't good for me nor me for them. Publishing is a particularly fertile ground for building relationships because we are involved, every day, with authors, booksellers and readers from diverse backgrounds.

The excitement of opening the door on these relationships may then be crowded out by rooms full of furnishings and designs which don't really do it for you.

A lack of alignment that will be hard to change. But the daily stimulus is there.

This is nowhere more evident than in the case of the trophy partner. Social media, Reality TV shows, celebrity magazines eulogise the partner as a trophy with all the complications that accompanies the concept.

I was at a publishing party in the River Room at the Savoy Hotel in London in the late '70s. The room was full of the great and the good and a colleague came up to me with great excitement that he had spied what he called 'a cracker' of a woman. Nick then proceeded to point out Gill, my wife at that time. I tell this story not as a conceit but because it illustrates how vulnerable we all are when we consider first appearances.

Some men make Oscar Wilde's shallowness only a millimetre deep as they respond to the stereotypical 'triggers' of the 'cracker' – the good-looking woman. What emerges is some kind of trade between men as to what you have got versus what I have got – diminishing our relationships to a list of bullet points of breasts, eyes, hair, crutch, bum and legs. The problem with this trade is that there can be a lot of money involved. In light of the gross gender inequality that affects the prospects of women and the burgeoning wealth of men – especially of the business and professional variety – the incentives for some women to acquiesce in the trophy wars are very high.

I am not suggesting that trophy-based relationships have to be unsuccessful but rather that their true value will not be apparent at the point of entry, if you follow my drift, only to become revealed as time passes by.

The gut-based nature of attraction is one of the great thrills in life. I can think of nothing more so than the anticipation of making love in the very near-future with the girl of your dreams. And the wonderful sense of release that follows – provided you have not had too many beers beforehand.

Our Love is Real

Yet I see you everywhere
Caring to turn a shadow
Into the depth of your eyes
And in the sky your hair
Is ruffled by an old wind
Yet I feel you everywhere
Firm between my legs
Neck kiss
Hands decking my chest, slow moving breast
And the warmth of such a paradise
Yet your smell is everywhere
Sitting on blue lines of smoke
Hiding in my beer
A drift down through my senses
Until all of you is here
I taste you, hear you too
Tongue folding with yours in soft darts
Quiet voices on whorled ears

When, tongue-tip moving,
Adventuring into this heady sphere
Yet because our love is real
These games sustain
Only till we meet again
Our bodies and minds making love
Carrying us along that tingling path
Lined with half-smiles, brown eyes and limbs
Mingling into a soft union of
Complete compatibility
. . . our love is real.

DULWICH, 1973

I don't believe that the nature of attraction is an aspect of a relationship which inevitably changes over time. It's usual to argue that the flush that comes when love blooms, dissipates over time. And I am well aware of many men of my age who have accepted making love three or four times a year based on the timing suggested by their partners. But the regularity and enjoyment of love-making is not just dependent on physical aspects such as ageing but on a clump of influences in which the physical aspects play a part. The most important of these is empathy. Your ability to understand and actively support your partner's emotional life, however tiresome it may sometimes be, and to recognise that generosity is the ultimate unit of currency that we share and not other people's views about who we are, or our sense of self-esteem. The late Andrew Fisher was part of the Oz

Magazine gang whose interests have criss-crossed with mine over the years. He worked with me in the 'eighties on a coffee table monster we put together for Richard Walsh, then publisher at Consolidated Press, called *The Australian Adventure*. Andrew enjoyed publishing and I asked him what he liked most about the industry. Frankly, he said he enjoyed the glamour that comes with the territory, asserting that, however dull the daily grind in the office, the high-profile media-hype made it all worthwhile. He further argued that when it came to domestic considerations you do best to leave the glamorous at work and accept a more muted home-life.

COMMITMENT

An enduring observation having watched men in relationships for over 50 years is their fear of commitment and a lack of understanding how important it is from their partner's point of view. To be honest, I think my problem has been the inverse. That I swing into total commitment mode at a moment's provocation when a studious approach would be more productive – and fairer on my partners.

Nevertheless, 'hook-phobia' is all around us. Perhaps, it is linked to the idea of playing the field so that you don't want to be tied down with one person when there may be better or simply more relationships to hand. But it goes deeper than that. It's not just a stance that you might adopt when they are young and unattached. It's a behaviour trait that lingers even when people are co-habiting or 'going steady'. The outward sign of commitment is not always supported by an inward pledge.

The institution of marriage, same-sex or otherwise, plays an interesting role here. Certainly, for my generation (I have to admit that I am too old even to be a baby-boomer!), our life-cycle included marriage, usually in our twenties and with very few of us co-habiting. And I have always seen marriage as that outward sign of an inward commitment. So, when Susie became pregnant with our first child, I was very keen to get married. Susie, a decade younger than me, did not see it that way at all – rejecting my proposal more than once. But her rejection was not a matter of commitment, as I would see it, but just a matter of choice.

We did marry before our eldest was born; perhaps Susie got tired of my nagging but the point is it was not a commitment issue from her point of view. This shift in the role of marriage is exaggerated by the behaviour of my seven children. Only three have married with Tom's first marriage ending in divorce. These days not marrying is as much the rule as marrying.

Commitment is also a significant attribute in publishing. It is perhaps most significant in the relationship between authors, their agents and the commissioning editor/publisher in the publishing house. Many authors will follow their editor/publisher whichever company they work for. Robert Gottlieb famously edited the novels of John Le Carre, Toni Morrison and Joseph Heller.

RESPECT

The measure of this topic indicates the ability of the couple to offer space and value to each other whatever their contributions may be to society at large. Without it, equality in a relationship becomes hard to achieve. Respect is not something to which lip-service is an adequate behaviour. It works best when it is not something said but when it informs our actions.

A thankfully now distant ex-in-law couple of mine were plagued by the misogynous contempt he displayed towards his partner, usually publicly communicated by his telling you how stupid she was. It was like an infection. And it broke out over the most trivial matters such as the thickness of a slice of bread, the parking of a car, the folding of a shirt. Apart from the air of unpleasantness that surrounded his behaviour, was her growing lack of self-esteem which was low at best but became rock-bottom once he got going. The outcome of his bullying has been the complete disempowerment of his partner – to the extent that if she contemplated moving out, she would not know where to start. She might even not know where the back-door was.

This example is an aspect of emotional abuse that usually lurks behind closed doors and which is so prevalent in the experiences of women in many traditional marriage settings. And when you do witness its public face, beware as there is often worse to follow.

Susie and I bicker a great deal but it's skin deep. We have a huge respect for each other which is not discussed as much as whose turn is it to clean out the fridge or why can't you put your clothes away when you are not using them and surely you can finish the sentence you started about half an hour ago?

COLLABORATION

A marriage close to me went awry after about 40 years. It was a great surprise to everyone involved as the outward signs gave no inkling of what had just happened. But apparently the internal dynamics had been off for years and the break-up from the point of view of one party was inevitable.

As we learned more about what had gone wrong it became apparent that the collaborative content of a life lived together was very low with the unhappy partner taking increasing refuge in pursuits that excluded the partner.

The reality of people co-habiting but living separate lives is all around us. And for great patches of time in my first marriage to Liz I was really good at doing my own thing. Weekend sports occupied heaps of my leisure time with their pubs, clubs and social events offering me a continuous source of entertainment. Matching that was a very busy working environment in publishing with its own socialising activities and distractions. Liz, meanwhile, carried on running the home with hardly a murmur but, in retrospect, as a sole homemaker (as experienced by so many young mothers) for much of the time – a role she was to undertake bravely and single-handedly after I left.

It is a measure of how different things can be when, with my third family underway, Saturdays were no longer taken up with me driving my kids to watch me play cricket in Oxford or Cambridge and plying them with crisps (oh all right . . . chips if you must!) through the car window in the pub car park, but with me driving my latest kids to their football and cricket matches in and around the Lower North Shore in Sydney.

I believe it is not only healthy to play sports but also for partners to have separate interests that are mutually supported in the context of a busy family life. These domains, however, need to be supported in a collaborative framework. This framework suggests that we do what we do because we both have the same freedoms and that we want to help each other lead a fulfilling life.

The underlying virtue of collaboration is the sense that 'we are in it together', that it is you and me against the world. But it is not only about sharing but also about building.

What seems to be apparent about this list of the virtues that make for a successful relationship is, in fact, how small each of them is. The little things that are as important as the big ones – particularly in the management of the psychological minutiae of family life.

I have excised from it such things as ambition and monetary success, a focus on physical beauty, social class and status, material acquisitions. We spend a great deal of time worrying about these big-ticket items but they don't quite make it as the building blocks for successful relationships.

Intimacy as we shall see is not only about sex, drugs, and rock and roll but much less!

To see a World in a Grain of Sand
And a Heaven in a Wild Flower
Hold Infinity in the palm of your hand
And Eternity in an hour
William Blake

Playlist

Eric Clapton, Wonderful Tonight
Roxy Music, A Song for Europe
Rolling Stones, Let's Spend the Night Together
The Pretenders, I'll Stand by You
The Beatles, Here Comes the Sun
Nick Cave & the Bad Seeds, Stranger than Kindness
Roy Orbison, I'll Say it's My Fault
Tony Bennett, The Good Life
The Cure, Pictures of You
The Beatles, Baby You Can Drive My Car
Sade, Your Love is King
Janis Joplin, Trust
Nirvana, Smells Like Teen Spirit
Cat Stevens, Wild World
Fairground Attraction, Perfect
Joe Cocker, You Are So Beautiful To Me
The Monkees, I'm A Believer
Gwen Stefani, The Real Thing
Peter Sellers, My Old Dutch

Stanley Holloway, Get Me To The Church On Time
Otis Redding, Respect
Roy Orbison, Only the Lonely
Nick Kershaw, These Little Things
Small is Beautiful, Video Killed the Radio Star

4

PASSION AND ROMANTIC LOVE

Sonnet

Who can plant the strands of his desires
in the paled region of logic's world?
Who can match the straightened line
with the dark fury of one life's moment?
Who can raise this tower of learning
In the rain-driven squall of passion's leap
And build his world from mind and matter,
ponderously fashioned in a compromised sleep?
With the fall of your beating breast
By the warmth of your softened face
To the curled tension of hearing's nest
And your splendid mouth of carmine grace
Along the margent of your thighs
In the shadows of your eyes

WIVENHOE, 1967

Falling *in* love feels like an absolute experience. It's a place we visit only occasionally and, when we do, it feels like a place we have been flung into from an ejector seat, triggered by someone else, without a parachute and without so much as a 'by your leave'. It's a scary place too as we often feel out of control with an object of our desire that is all-embracing, somebody we really want to consume. This aspect I think of as the 'amoeba-kiss'. We want our embrace to surround completely the physicality of the loved-one so we can absorb them into our own being. Two now one. These tell-tale signs may never be part of your life. Social convention as in arranged marriages or marriages which tick boxes are ever present. And I have many friends who, without social pressure, are happily married but where being extrovertly 'in love' is now and probably always has been absent.

My first experience of being in love was with Liz, my first wife. We had an idyllic start to our relationship in a country setting in Hampshire. The unique quality of my experience of love with Liz was enhanced by my role, soon after we got back together, acting the part of Lysander in *A Midsummer Night's Dream* which The Magdalen Players staged in the Deer Park at my college, in the summer of 1964. Love was the drug even if it was promoted not by Bryan Ferry but by Oberon and his cohorts and we were its prey!

This desire for unity (maybe this is what passion is about) creates an unsteady state, too. Its psychological frame might be summed up as separation anxiety. Why not list for yourself the mad things you have done when you have been in love? Mad and maybe sometimes bad! Why else would I walk through the 1964 blizzards and snow drifts, recovering from a dislocated knee operation, to Shalden, the village where Liz lived, when all of Hampshire's transport systems had come to an ungritty halt. Or even to spend an extra thousand of my own dollars to bring my homeward flight from Silicon Valley to Sydney a day earlier than booked so as to fast-track the reunion with Susie.

The Beatles captured this aspect of love arguing in the song *My Life* that the person you are in love with reigns supreme and the importance of longevity as a component of being in love.

—

For my love and my money, it's the most profound emotional state we encounter short of the often-unexpected journeys we make on the birth of our children or the death of family members. Every 'frisson' in the 'in love' relationship – a shared glance across a room; the quick phone call between appointments; giggling; the bunch of flowers at the front door; replaying again and again, the current pop-song – is an investment that acts as a signpost to a promised eternity that leaves us spellbound and wondering what could possibly come next.

When Liz and I push-biked and walked three or four miles home from Alton in Hampshire to Shalden after an absorbing evening with Long John Baldry (or was it Alexis Corner?) at *The Wooden Bridge* in Guildford (the members to be of the, then, unknown Rolling Stones would occasionally jam during the break between sets) it was as if the whole world stood still. Or Gill and I giggling involuntarily in The *Duke of York* pub near Lords cricket ground in St John's Wood on our way to deliver her home from a day's publishing work on an airfield in Hertfordshire; or Susie and I meeting to postpone our relationship at The Oaks in Neutral Bay on a sultry spring evening that ended up with our agreeing to move in together as soon as possible.

The 'in love' experience has built within it an extraordinary range of powers. Its release destroys any doubts as to its reality and it is a destructive force for many men who are swept away on the tide of excitement to reject their past for an immersive present.

Time freezes as these moments become an act of homage to your feelings. There's no need to work on mindfulness and presence when you are in love because the experience comes fully-packaged without the need for any therapy. It really is all or nothing.

I do have one story to illustrate my comment about not needing therapy. Soon after I left Liz, Geoff who had been my best man at our wedding and was married to Liz's cousin, contacted me with therapy in mind. His view of which he informed most urgently was that I had gone mad and needed to see a shrink ASAP. We met in a pub in Wandsworth, appropriately called The Ram Inn. Geoff took the view that my love for Gill was a mental illness best dealt with by seeing a therapist. This view, that being in love is some sort of illness, is widespread. People find it hard to get inside your head and understand what is going on. I loved Geoff and that whole episode has been one of the great sadnesses of my life. I wrote a poem about it after Geoff died in 2005.

Ockyford

I never understood why your love for me
Was dependent upon my love for another
And when that love fell, as it always would,
That I'd lose you, my heart soul brother.
There's little to go on since we split in '73
Thirty years is doing time without cover
Lives change and co-mingle with new blood
Turning shared lives into being some other.
This heart's journey has been strong for you
Sending you photos, cards, like an ex-lover
Despite years of trying to re-open the wood,
I have lost you again, my heart soul brother.
Why have you died before reaching back for me?
Before we could hug like children with their mother?

The patient constancy of my feelings would
Have been rewarded, the waiting over.
So it won't be. They have put you to rest.
Dodgy plastic guts inside that once-red chest.
I remember you standing at the ocky
Leaning forward, dart-ready, ever so cocky.
There we were, pissed in the Old Bursary,
A bunch of kids barely out of nursery
And you all puissance and camaraderie
Wearing your dog tooth jacket, ginger of course,
And that scarf, throat-knotted as it flops,
The arrow on its way into double tops.
Did you understand the nature of my love for you?
It was not dependent upon my love for another.
It has always been unconditional, like
    they say in the books,
Hear me now and sleep well, my heart soul brother.

SYDNEY, 2005

These scenes from my life endorse my learning that
every love affair is both the same *and* also different
from any other. This difference operates in two ways.
Not just in your own life but when compared with
experiences of those around you.

Firstly, these human experiences are both shared
and unique at the same time. Shared because we recognise that other people have gone through the same
things as I have but unique because when it happens
to me there is no way you can know exactly what I am

thinking and feeling. Think about the first death of a parent; or feel the pain of losing your job after trying so hard; or being teased and bullied online or burgled at home.

Second, because in the chronology of our life, the love affair I am having now robs all past affairs of their uniqueness. It's worth noting, that this transition does not rob your past affairs of value but it changes the dynamics of that value from the absolute (you are the only one for me) to the relative (you're not the only person in the world).

A family member went through a surprising marriage break-down after 40 years. What followed was World War Three with no prisoners. Epistemology (what we know) becomes the prisoner of ontology (how we know) as we, the players in the drama, are flung into metaphysical territories that are unbearably new. How on earth did I get here, we ask ourselves, as rationality flies out of the window. The bastard!

This is the characteristic journey that accompanies being in love – absolute one day, relative the next – and is the crux that informs this book. And as we all may know, we move from one 'state' to another by the sort of questions we ask of ourselves. Be honest, how many times have you said, looking back on your ended relationship, (particularly if you were the antagonist!), I had no idea that there could be one better. Ironically, that idea is not immediate. I think it takes about two years to recover from a break-up whichever side of the activity-fence you happen to inhabit. Dealing with unexpected moments like calling your new partner by your ex's name (so embarrassing if your making love at that time!), looking at the step-children you have inherited and wondering how the hell can they be so cold towards you, or stumbling on mementos around the house that belong to that bygone era.

The toughest challenge given this line of thought is remembering that the sidelined relationship was once absolute. Thus, we need, if we can, to honour the person involved even though we have moved ahead. I think I have done that across my three marriages, or at least tried to. I am over-bearingly self-confident (how else could I write this book?! Was it Oscar Wilde who said 'to fall in love with yourself is the beginning of a lifelong romance'), which helps, and I have never attempted to rationalise where I want to be now by reinterpreting what it was like to be where I was then. My feelings, by way of example, towards Liz are simple. The love we shared and our three children are more precious now than, from my point of view, they were at the time. The often encountered need to bad-mouth the person you have dumped must be resisted. It's understandable, however, because we often feel the need to rationalise our behaviour in the context of negative responses from family and friends.

These negative responses can often arrive in strange ways. When my first marriage ended in 1974 a close friend of both Liz and myself, rang me to meet me for a drink. We went to the *John Snow* in Soho, next door to where I was working for Granada Publishing, which in those days was the home for weekly meetings of the Harry Lauder Society and a favourite venue for publishers and local writers like Colin MacInnes.

My good friend, Barry, from Granada TV's *World in Action* team, wanted to know why I had not been supporting Liz and my three young children financially following the break-up. Well I had. In fact, I am proud to say that I have never once not honoured my financial obligations to the adults caught up in my two failed marriages and the four children from them. Proud, yes, but it should not be any other way. The source of Barry's concern was, as it turned out, general disapproval from some of my friends at my leaving the first family and the understandable need for people to give me a good dressing down.

One of the hard lessons of a breakdown is that so many people see you so much as being part of a couple that they cannot focus on you as an individual. True friends can transcend this problem without feeling a need to take sides. But it's usually messy and difficult to manage. The internal dynamics of family gatherings are a case in point. When my first marriage ended I moved from being a senior wrangler to an often-uninvited occupant below the salt and it took years (and a successful relationship) for my customary role to be renewed.

It's worth pointing out at this stage that, in

retrospect, it is really difficult to understand the decisions we take in the heat of the moment; especially where young children are involved. And the perplexity of these occasions is doubled by something like a Catch-22. You shouldn't leave and you couldn't stay. It is no wonder that I have found that the role of the protagonist (the leaver) is in so many ways harder than the role of the antagonist (the left).

Acknowledging the trauma of separation, I have managed to stay friends with my past-loves despite the passions which swirled around their breakdown. On my fiftieth birthday 'surprise' party underneath the Sydney Harbour Bridge and then at North Sydney Oval, Susie made a delightful speech to celebrate my half-century. She said that with regard to my ex-wives and girl-friends how odd it was that I remained friends with them all, ever after. 'However,' she concluded 'please note, not one of them is here tonight!' Good girl!

One of my closest male friends has lived with his life partner putting in play two of the most disempowering features of the way men can treat women. First, he celebrates womanhood as some kind of idealised existence which puts his partner on a pedestal as a princess who moves through the rites of passage like a heroine in a fairy story – initially a vulnerable virgin, then a rescued romantic, followed by marriage, the miracle of childbirth and a life of service to her husband and family. Eyelids fluttering, she accepts the role of the adored sexual object without seeing the demeaning impact of this archetype on her soul, her social contribution, her potential fulfilment as a human being.

The second feature was the narrow reality of daily life for women. The 'domestic' rites of passage – from partner, to mother, to housewife – were seen to be inalienable. Just as its opposite (the 'pedestal' effect I have just outlined) created an illusion of achievement so the 'housewife' effect destroyed the possibility of charting a unique pathway through life.

Things have changed somewhat in the last 50 years but we live in a (western) world where the views that have shaped the way women are seen are deeply etched in the way power is distributed between the sexes. It is after all, Kate Millett argued in *Sexual Politics* (which I was also involved with publishing for Rupert Hart-Davis in the UK), the political underpinning of the way we see the world that is so pernicious and divisive.

Romantic love, in the traditional sense of it, has been the relationship driver in my life. My first and last loves, Liz and Susie, not to mention Gill, were each as equally consuming as each other. When I fall in love it is a total experience to the exclusion of everyone and, at times, anything else unfortunately including children. My latest love affair is always a surprise, not just because it happened, but because I can't understand how it could be better than the one it has eclipsed. And this new love feels as if it must last for ever. I note that my views are based on my role as a protagonist rather than being the person set aside. You might also note that I have assumed that it's OK to move on to the next relationship as if it's an inexorable process. Obviously, it isn't and some of the happiest relationships I have witnessed around me have been for life. Indeed, the participants to one such relationship that I have been alongside for over 50 years quite simply become more beautiful as the years tick by.

Returning to my theme, a month before Gill walked into my life in late 1973, I was in New York – it was the time of the Yom Kippur War. Fund raising rallies brought New York's Jewish community onto the streets and into Central Park as I was visiting US publishers on behalf of Granada Publishing. The three-week trip was dragging; New York can be a hostile environment even for mad dogs and Englishmen. I remember writing letters home to Liz (we'd been married now for almost a decade with three young children) avowing my undying love for her, each letter sealed with a real kiss.

But within three months of returning to London that love had been swamped by the tide of feelings I felt for Gill. Every love affair in which I have participated is informed by the idea that this affair is more important than any affair that preceded it. And that it will last for ever.

When, after Gill and I got together in the UK, on one of my many trips to Toronto, I fell in love with Valerie, who hailed from Montreal. So powerful was the feeling of being in love with her that on one occasion, en route via Canada for a summer holiday in Australia,

I travelled from Toronto to Montreal just to see Valerie.

I was wearing a summer outfit suitable for Bondi in December when the Canadian winter was in full blast with the wind-chill factor bringing the temperature down to -18C. It was so cold that my beard froze as I waited to get on the plane.

This way of living which consumed me between the ages of 20 and 40 was inimical to the development of a sustainable intimate relationship. And bad news for those involved. The architecture of intimacy is not built on such an unstable foundation. It does not thrive if one of the parties is likely to turn their back on it for something new. Romantic love needs more, and is more, than the passion I have been describing.

There's a dialectic at work in the nature of romantic love. Because its thesis demands a relationship to be absolute, unique, and forever the seeds for its downfall are already in place. Human progress cannot survive in such an environment. Our lives are contextual. Relative not absolute; comparative not unique; temporary not infinite. Once any of these antithetical truths enter a relationship (which they must) the concept of romantic love collapses.

We can see that romantic love is not sustainable. The challenge is not to be blind about the nature of reality but rather to change the way we see it. Nor does it suggest (as the theme of this book attempts to show) that what replaces it is inferior. Far from it. True intimacy, as I hope to show, is the great provider. This is the destination for what starts as romantic love.

Accepting that new view of reality means you are only a step away from discovering the pathway to intimacy. Acceptance can take many forms. One example from my life is a conversation I had with one of my children who was, and still is, in a long-term relationship with his childhood sweetheart. Given my experience with Liz, my first wife (who is not his mum, by the way) who had been my childhood sweetheart, I questioned his wisdom in not playing the field before settling down.

He told me that it was all OK because she was not only his lover, but his best friend. I replay this conversation again and again. Why did it take me 25 years to work this out when my son twigged it very early on? I think, above everything, I had been a ruthless pleasure seeker, incapable of seeing the damage caused to intimacy as being irreversible. I always assumed I could get away with it and that my virtues would outweigh the vices. This flawed attitude was exacerbated by my alpha-male ego exploiting the privileges and opportunities I enjoyed and an ingrained need to get my own way, to do what I want and the devil take the hindmost.

Harry had got in a trice what it took me a quarter of a century to discover.. The emotional intelligence embedded in his response is an object lesson for cynics and pessimists who see relationships as harbingers of disappointment and sadness. Their idea is along the lines that being in love is a form of infatuation that will be crucified by reality and will survive only on the shoulders of compromise. What my son was saying is that the poetry of romantic love can be enriched by the more prosaic text of friendship – not as a substitute for true love but as its protector. Friendship rules.

Romantic love, for all its attractions, is deeply connected to sexual politics. It is the fulcrum on which we have built the nuclear family as an ideal system for our social development. And it patterns deeply our sense of what really matters in relationships.

Women in particular are deeply involved in its impact on their lives. It is not surprising that women are the main audience for all types of media that promote, investigate and reflect on romantic love. ('olde time' authors like Mary Stewart, Georgette Heyer and Daphne du Maurier are almost exclusively read by women as are contemporaries like Marian Keyes, Katie Foord and Danielle Steel).

The role of romance in literary lives is not about escapism. But it does convey a deep mistrust of the its role in real life. Having lived my 'real' life as a serial monogamist (well, most of the time!), I must admit to being attracted by the notion of romantic love but for me its corollary is not an idealised 'happy ever after . . . The End' but the hard-won achievement of a true intimacy with an exclusive partner of mutual choice.

I hope what I have been saying is not psycho-babble. The delight of writing this book is that it is a learning process for me as I try to work out how the hell I got, in my eighties, to be living in a foreign country with kids on two continents and grand-children popping out here there and everywhere and sharing my life for the last forty years with someone who was introduced to me, after Gill had cut and run, by a close friend asking 'would you like to meet the nicest girl in Australia?' Of course I said 'no'. But as it turned out he was right!

The next chapter explores aspects of the link between the poetic and the prosaic.

Playlist

Tame Impala, Desire Be, Desire Go
Roxy Music, Love Is the Drug
The Beatles, In My Life
Sinead O'Connor, Nothing Compares 2 U
Coldplay, Death of a Friend
ZZ Top, Don't Tease Me
The Everly Brothers, Bye Bye Love
Ry Cooder, Alimony
Everly Brothers, Wake Up Little Susie
Sting, Fields of Gold
Neil Young, Heart of Gold
Queen, Love of My Life
The Dandy Warhols, Best Friend
Billy Joel, She's Always a Woman
Leonard Cohen, Famous Blue Raincoat

5

COMMITMENT AND PRAGMATISM

Famous Blue Raincoat

The bush fires have been raging
and delivering their load.
I'm wearing your hat,
as a gesture, now you're dead
and thinking of the litany
of women you have shed.
You see women as possessions,
not to be shared,
'other-touching' as transgression
and not topics to be aired.
Your definition of wife
is a monastic life
where freedom has gone
and chains now belong.

If you were to return,
I'd want to say 'hey!
What are you hiding
under your famous blue raincoat?
Your narrative has gone clear
but what about the fear
that you are never here
but lost forever in your
self-seeking stanzas
where love is a poem
that makes you feel grander.
It must be time for you
to launch a new boat
and toss into the water
your famous blue raincoat,
to take courage in your existence
as a hairy old goat.
It's beginning to rain.
Where is my brolly?
sincerely, Leonard,
your new friend,
Oli

BONDI, 2019

In an earlier chapter, I listed commitment as being one of the platforms on which true intimacy stands.

Commitment is an elusive state that has significant ramifications for relationships. Its positive meaning is around the idea of dedication to a cause, maybe in the form of a pledge or an undertaking. It connotes loyalty, exclusivity and even 'true love'. The marriage vows typify this with the words 'I do' spoken out loud to the congregation; an outward sign of an inward promise.

But like many of the ideas that I am touching on, there's a dark side to it, too. Many of us see such a resolution, not as Hamlet's '. . . consummation, devoutly to be wished', but as an obligation that restricts freedom of action and, thus, to be resisted at all costs. This point of view is a feature of the way many men approach relationships. It also connotes one of the trickiest implications of marriage – that what is traded is a property right. Indeed, the marriage contract and pre-nups are legal documents that focus on the property aspects.

I think my Oz friend Andrew loved his artist partner but there was no way that he would offer the commitment that she wanted and needed. The relationship dwindled and she was forced to give him up. Andrew was totally aware that this would be the outcome but could not act otherwise. When a pledge is wanted and not made, the relationship may be left to stumble along with partners not getting the commitment that they see as a basis for success. A shared commitment, in my book, is the first fence in the Intimacy Grand National! Of course, beware the reverse situation – when a pledge is made and not really wanted and signalled by the comment 'you are always saying that . . .'

These positive and negative implications of commitment are a rich thread throughout literature, balancing love as an infinite and unique resource on the one hand with love as a finite tradeable item on the other. TS Eliot and W Shakespeare are among many exemplars of this though from very different points of view.

> She turns and looks a moment in the glass,
> Hardly aware of her departed lover;
> Her brain allows one half-formed thought to pass:
> 'Well now that's done: and I'm glad it's over.'
> When lovely woman stoops to folly and
> Paces about her room again, alone,
> She smoothes her hair with automatic hand,
> And puts a record on the gramophone.
>
> T S ELIOT. THE WASTELAND

> My bounty is as boundless as the sea
> My love as deep;
> The more I give to thee
> The more I have
> For both are infinite
>
> W SHAKESPEARE, JULIET IN ROMEO & JULIET

There is a cultural context for the way we see commitment and the duties that it brings with it. In the '70s, as aspects of feminism became more general currency, there was some improvement in reducing gender stereotypes at home and in the workplace. But only some. Among my generation, male responsibilities in the workplace took precedence over sharing responsibilities at home, and still are prevalent, though slightly weaker, today. And in my case, being a powerful and ego-driven person, this dynamic catapulted me into the behaviours I have recounted above.

Employers have made some progress in this area but it's disappointing how slow it has been. A senior publishing colleague of mine working for a multinational publishing house in Sydney sought my views on how she could manage the company's failure to amend work-practices to meet her needs as a new mother. 'Why,' she asked 'do they pay lip-service to organisational change but then arrange meetings for 4.30 pm in the afternoon when I need to be back home looking after my infant bub?'

For reasons like this, the context in which commitment operates becomes a movable feast. The values and practices in the external environment define the requirements of commitment in your 'internal' relationship environment. Thus, the social impacts on the personal. When I reflect on my life I am increasingly aware how restricting is the pressure from outside but not to the extent of absolving me from being a pretty slow adaptor in times of change. Perhaps we are all delusional when thinking how we fit into a bigger picture.

Gender stereotyping is a major issue in the search for commitment. The stereotyping that we all encounter is an abstraction set in the outside world which affects the internal dynamics of relationships. My Lady-Tradie poem in celebration of my time with Susie expresses how the suspension of belief can help build a strong foundation.

Lady–Tradie

I thought our relationship
was about love and romance
that you were my first lady
and I wore the pants.
But then it emerged
sorry if I have to shout
that you are a lady-tradie.
This is what you're about
Two by twos and four by fours
You'll fix the taps, if I go shopping,
grout the tiles and hang the door
– even sand the deck without stopping.
Come to bed love, forget the flashing,
you know I think you are really smashing.

ROZELLE, 2017

Susie's view that I should not be allowed near an electric drill, hammer or pot of paint invites me to exploit her goodwill as to who is getting the jobs done. I am sure I am complicit in this but I can't be quite as bad as the official press release from *The Susie Morning Herald*. Nevertheless, we have together found things for me to do. After all, I shop and cook, tidy the spice rack and polish the silver and deal with the financial and admin aspects of running our home.

We have secured an understanding as to who does what and only come to blows when we feel the tension between myself as the 'collector' and Susie as the 'declutterer'. By way of example, I have started to collect flamingos, inspired by a chance Hawaiian shirt purchase from Lowes (the Aussie battler's store!) in Woy Woy. The flamingos can be in any form – jewellery, china, clothing etc – and are beginning to take shape as a collection in my 'room of unearthly delights', a room Susie does not enter willingly because it is so full of . . . stuff. I have also recently added a glass display cabinet to house my smaller knick-knacks.

Despite raised eyebrows, Susie recognises that I have substantially reduced my collections via Lawsons' auctions and gifts to family members and, who knows, when I shuffle off she will be able finally ring Lawson's to say, 'Have I got a sale for you!' and to reduce them all to a few photos on her laptop.

The ability to trade points of view, needs and what we offer each other is at the heart of commitment. This is the give and take of learning how to relate with another human being for the long-term. In pragmatic terms managing commitment is not easy.

For me, there are dangers and unexpected hazards which we encounter every day. Maslow's hierarchy of needs goes someway to helping us engage with the curly bits of relationships by revealing the tensions that exist quite naturally in our psychological make-ups.

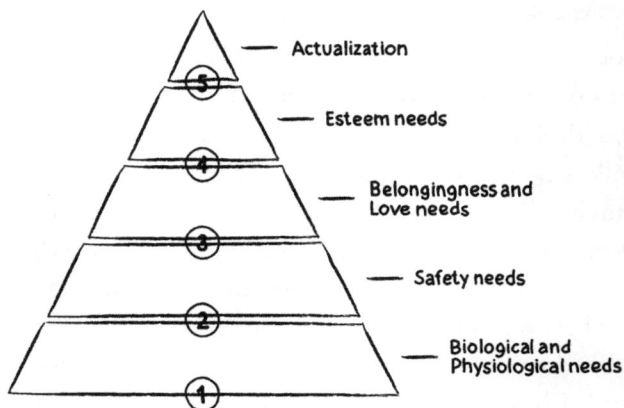

It's not my purpose to debate the relevance of the content of Maslow's thinking but rather to focus on some aspects of its process. What intrigues me is the notion that our development as human beings contextualises all the things that I am talking about as being relative to each other. Take a look at my chapter headings and you may see what I see – a list of behavioural characteristics that are not mutually exclusive but which interplay with each other as we make the journey (with luck) from teenagers and young adults prospecting and playing the field to old chooks enjoying true intimacy. But, unlike Maslow's scheme, it is not linear. Most of the steps on the way between the start and finish lines appear disappear and reappear in any order at any time.

The movie *Two for the Road* (yes, I know that dates me good and proper), starring Albert Finney and Audrey Hepburn analyses what happens in a relationship that started off as romantic love and is now both familiar and tense as life goes by. One of the more profound responses to this journey is a most important takeaway. In a permanent love relationship, whatever the ups and downs, when you take stock at any moment it is not just about the 'now'. It is about everything that precedes the 'now' as well. This explains why when couples break up protagonists have a strong desire to negate the history of the relationship in favour of the 'now' while the antagonists do the opposite. They endorse the content of the past and reject the 'now'.

A key feature of the committed partner is, therefore, learning to both anticipate and understand how these behavioural aspects might play out. And this understanding includes that there are moments when, for example, your loss of control in the situation, is an inevitable consequence of the complexities of all relationships. Temperamentally, men often think all problems in their relationships are their problems. So, when their partner is blue, they want to intervene and fix it. But many problems have nothing to do with them and the best course of action is to do nothing and wait for it to blow over.

Spare a moment for the in-laws in relationships, a role I have fulfilled sixteen times so far. The role is at best a win-lose one but often a lose/lose. My seven children have been quite normal in developing relationships which succeed or fail whatever the perturbations. We engage with their partners to provide support and encouragement in pursuit of a happy outcome. But then it all goes wrong and the love we have nurtured for their ex-partner is marooned with nowhere to go. We feel helpless as the person we have grown to love and commit to is whisked off the chessboard. Queen or pawn, it matters not. This is yet another source of grief in this messy life we have constructed together. It won't be all right in the end, whatever Fernando Sabino or John Lennon may say. But it will be different.

The love we may have developed for our partners or the partners of our children often feels as if it is unconditional. We often speak warmly about our canine pets that their major virtue is providing unconditional love – even if it is obsequiousness in disguise! We all want the love people have for us to be unconditional but absolutely everything about the institution of marriage (or permanent partnering for that matter) suggests the opposite – that our relationships are conditional and that there is a contract that is at least implicit if not expressed in a pre-nuptial agreement. It is also a fact of life that, sometimes, unconditional love hasn't a hope of consummation as every Mills & Boon reader knows.

The title of this chapter tells the same story. We ask for absolute commitment but the pragmatic aspects of our relationships are built on the understanding that there is a great deal of give and take in the way we manage them.

There is, perhaps, a way through the conflict of commitment and pragmatism which, I hope, is more than a semantic twist. As a parallel to what I want to say, think for a moment about mortality. Having done my three score years and ten, I have learned that we like to live our lives as if we are immortal. Time and again, I have been in situations where the reality of mortality suddenly comes into view, perhaps for a friend diagnosed with cancer, a parent being consumed by dementia, parents of a child run over by a car. These often-abrupt circumstances reveal the ticking clock which patterns all our lives.

Trial by Life

My Welsh neurologist
Is full of fun as we address
The complex symptoms
Of life's egress
It seems to me certain
My life is mortal
Each year taking me nearer
To the exit portal
Loss of smell
Quivering hands
Disturbed sleeping
Equivocal scans

Chest pains
Slow walking
Creeping deafness
Look who's talking!
There is a deathly truth –
Like a Rorschach blot –
If you live long enough
You'll just get the lot.

ROZELLE, 2018

This erroneous belief in immortality will not disappear for everyone. Members of new generations coming through will make the same journey as I have. And it is not a journey without positive outcomes. The instinct to fight for survival, the ambition to achieve goals, the desire for improvement in the way we live our lives are all based on the strengths that are delivered by what Wordsworth describes in *Intimations of Immortality*.

But trailing clouds of glory do we come
From God, who is our home:
Heaven lies about us in our infancy!

It's almost as if the idea of our souls being immortal is part of the innocence we have as children and that growing up is a loss of this innocence in exchange for the reality of mortality.

What might all this mean for relationships? Yes, you guessed! They are both absolute/unconditional and relative/pragmatic at the same time. This apparent paradox lies at the heart of all our human values. We honour them individually as being indivisible but we know that if we take them as a whole that some values are more absolute than others. So we may well, as Old Major suggest in George Orwell's *Animal Farm*, all be born equal but some of us are more equal than others. It is the major feature of the human condition that we pick our way through the values minefield and seek ways of living that accommodate both states.

Returning to Maslow for a moment, the notion of a hierarchy of conditions turns out to be relevant. We can't be all things to everyone simultaneously. We have to choose what is most important for us in our relationships and to carry these value-flags under the banner of unconditional love. The dialectical tension that values in conflict can create is the stuff that the human condition delivers. And we only need reflect on the ups and downs of our relationships to see how this might work out.

When I fell in love with Gill, my love for Liz lost its supremacy and the conflict then arose between the new love and my love for my children. Ten years later Gill's love for someone better at cricket than me relegated my love to the second eleven and affected yet another child whose well-being became a casualty of the adults' intentions.

My experience tells me that it is only by going through family breakdowns that we learn how to manage them – to be pragmatic about a commitment under attack. The introduction of children into my reflections is inevitable because I have never had a permanent relationship without children. I suspect that the emotional turmoils of breakdown without children are just as harrowing but pragmatically speaking somewhat easier to manage.

Playlist

. . . .

Dire Straits, Lady Writer
Eric Clapton, Wonderful Tonight
Lily James, I Have a Dream
Cindi Lauper, Time After Time
Manfred Man, Pretty Flamingo
The Righteous Brothers, Unchained Melody
Bruce Springsteen, Two for the Road
Maroon 5, Nobody's Love
The Beatles, When I'm Sixty Four
Bob Dylan, Time Passes Slowly
Celine Dion/Bee Gees, Immortality
Mindy Carson, You Can't be True to Two

6

WEDDINGS AND
GETTING TOGETHER

Would You Like To . . .?

Would you like to lose the spontaneity
    which graced our first meeting,
(Making each after-day an adventure
    of emotions, of exploration)
and the gut sinking, fast blinking laughter of it all?
Would you like to trade your independence
(Looking for the signs, misleading,
    rereading, not seeing)
for the interdependency we promised
    as new meaning?
Would you like to stay at home
    while I am out to play,
(Wondering about fulfilment as the
    angry voices sound)

nurse my children and my ego, do
    the domestic round?
Would you like to see a spectre of the
    future in the albums of my past,
(Listening to the song lines of my family
    with patience and grace)
Searching and searching for your very own place?
Will you marry me?

CREMORNE, 2002

Wedding ceremonies in my experience, and I have had a few, are some of the strangest events in our social calendar. They are built on a dynamic that seems to be the opposite of reality. And that dynamic is one of a presumed symmetry of the relationships between the couple approaching the altar. Let me take you back to the modest Anglican church of St Peter & St Paul in Shalden Hampshire (where Liz lived) in the diocese of Winchester and part of the united Benefice of Shalden, Medstead, Bentworth and Lasham (where I lived). It is 19 September 1964 and Liz and I are about to get married.

The church is fairly full with my family and friends arranged on the groom's side of the church and the bride's pews, to the left, housed those of Liz's. Bride, groom, left, right, my best man, Geoff who I have mentioned before, and Liz's father right and left – everything about the ceremony was based on symmetry. The coming together of two equals to share the wedding vows with the congregation. The identical wedding vows (once the word 'obey' had been excised from the wife's pledges) are made by bride and groom. The liturgy was familiar to everyone despite my Freudian slip when I summoned 'the son, the father and the Holy Ghost' to bless us in the usual way!

The symmetrical dynamic of the ceremony, however, runs counter to the experience of the marriage that follows. Not just for Liz and me but pretty well every couple in Christendom. In my book, the most challenging aspect of marriage is managing the innate asymmetry that governs the lives of the protagonists *after* the visit to the registry office or after they have journeyed down the aisle and greeted the new day with the ringing of church bells and throwing of confetti from well-wishers all.

In our case, our journeys were knocked out of reciprocity by Liz's role as a mother-to-be with three babies to be born over the next seven years while mine was preoccupied with the rapid promotion in my career as a publisher and, as explained earlier, my lack of a deep nuclear family experience in matters to do with relationships of all kinds.

Whatever the specific details driving asymmetry, there is no doubt that the participants in a marriage develop at different rates from each other. When Liz and I started out, she was literally in the driving seat coming from a wealthy upper-middle-class family compared with the penny-pinching Bohemian milieu that housed me. She had a driver's licence and access to cars to take us around in to pubs and parties. Chauffeuse and hostess with the mostest, Liz provided a great foundation for our social life. But marriage and three babies later, and I am now in the driving seat; the source of cash and cars with an expansive job in publishing that was taking me to Europe and the US while she was at home managing our young family and wondering how our roles had reversed. Not just totally but so quickly.

The role of asymmetry in marriage is offset to a degree by the concept of being part of a 'couple'. Coupledom was raised emphatically by John Updike in his '60s novel, *Couples*, about ten couples in the US whose behaviours both question and endorse the idea of the social and sexual bond between partners. Certainly, in London at that time, when many of us were struggling to understand how to respond to the way the world had changed since the '50s of our childhood, could we maintain our role as couples while exploring open marriage? Just what did sexual liberation mean for us as pillars of society, as parents and as friends?

The traction provided by coupledom was very strong and still is today. When Liz and I separated in 1974, I remember only too well that many of our friends could not come to terms with the 'decoupling' that I had initiated – I was part of 'Oliver and Liz' and not 'Oliver' on my own. It is perplexing how the social milieu adds to the difficulties of separation, especially for the protagonists, who are like little boats set adrift on the choppy waters of opprobrium. When Gill separated from me, the experience was altogether different as we had just arrived in Sydney after a decade in London. We were not an established couple with couple-friends so the journey was somewhat easier. And my emotional situation was mitigated somewhat by meeting Susie just two weeks after Gill went back to the UK.

We spend most of our adult lives operating in two theatres. One is the theatre of employment which occupies anything from 35 to 50 hours a week (and even more if you are entrepreneurial as was I in the last 30 years of employment). The other is the nuclear family which houses most of us for about 70 hours a week – thus leaving 50 hours or so for sleep!

I have always been attracted to the 'good life' – to drugs, sex and rock and roll. But just how do you fit that in with the duties and timetables outlined above?

As a young and relatively poor dad (I was just 21 on a student grant when Tom was born) it seemed unlikely that I would be living that life from home. I was much later given some very poor advice about this dilemma by my Aussie friend Andrew who, you may remember, suggested I should not look for glamour in my family life but, instead, seek it out in my business domain.

I am not sure I have followed the advice to the full but there is absolutely no doubt that the tension between my family and business roles played a big part in the failure of my marriage to Liz and had some bearing on the difficulties I encountered with Gill.

This was not just the significant overseas travel with a healthy expense account that accompanied my job as Managing Director of the law publishers, Oyez Publishing, but also time spent wining and dining when I was in London at times when Liz could have done with my support in feeding the kids and getting them to bed.

In parallel to this idea, I remember a session with my financial adviser, Chris, as we prepared to go to a meeting in London with Coutts Bank in The Strand. 'In summary, Oliver, you are a successful publisher with three children and you own your own house in Dulwich – but you can't afford to buy a loaf of bread.' I nodded. We went in to negotiate the third mortgage with the class-conscious bank's executive, dapperly dressed in top hat and tails, providing much needed funds.

These opposites I explored in marriage and family – symmetrical engagement / asymmetrical personal development; business wealth / home poverty; grinding domesticity / glamourous international travel – are not gender neutral. Perhaps the strongest driver of asymmetry in the marriage world of my youth is that 90%–95% of the leading business roles were filled by men. One consequence of this was that the cult of leadership in business and government was built around men in such a way that the resulting inequalities were reflected in the more general attitudes to the roles of men and women in society.

Women were seen to be providers of domestic services to marriages which, in turn, men used as a springboard to develop their careers. And, surprise, surprise the social roles available for women who did not want to stay at home and mind the kids were the more domestic or child-centred ones – nursing, teaching, librarianship, cleaning, community care and so on. Please note that I am not belittling these professions but noting that the range of occupational options for women was limited and is only now beginning to expand.

Of course, things have changed in the last 50 years and the percentage of women in senior executive roles has grown to around 30% as have creche -type services. But there is still a long way to go.

These values which pattern social institutions like marriage are not there by chance. They reflect the way, for example, the distribution of power 'distorts' what we might regard as an ideal outcome for the people involved. Most men in the 2020s still see their roles taking precedence over the domestic roles that family life requires. Of course, this is less so than 55 years ago when I started work. But the underlying assumptions are stubborn and hard to shift. Ironically, the idea of a 'stay at home dad' perpetuates the problem rather than liberates it. What about 'stay at home mums'!

I'd like to add another layer to these difficulties. As argued earlier I have always believed in the institution of marriage. Despite my weakness for swapping rings, I have no problems with three of my children seeing marriage as an unnecessary element in their long-term relationships.

As I have said, the presumption of symmetry that the wedding ceremony suggests is false. Neither is the assumed symmetry just about relationships, it is also about property. The coming together of two families in the form of the betrothed who bring to the union actual property or rights to property. Ask Jerry Hall as she divorces Rupert Murdoch!

The tacit agreement at this point, if there is no 'pre-nup' stating otherwise, is usually that each partner owns what they bring to the marriage and, thereafter, property increases are shared equally between them. And once more these assumptions exaggerate the asymmetry in the relationships between couples rather than underlining a supposed equality.

There is, of course, more to relationships than those things suggested by looking at the human history of institutions like marriage. Wedding ceremonies are becoming less universal and when they do exist the differences for example between Jewish, Greek, Indian and Inuit weddings are substantial.

From the standpoint of intimacy, the underlying theme for this book, the critical idea behind marriage is 'getting together'. But we have all witnessed friends and relatives in relationships where being together is weak or absent. If I reflect on my three marriages each is so different on this score. One is shaped by a profound sense of being together which is probably why it is still rocking after 40 years. One had aspects of togetherness but where the interaction between the two of us was highly competitive so 'together' morphed to 'against' and my first marriage which went from the positive together gear into the neutral 'absent' model, getting ready for a shift into reverse.

So, togetherness means different things at different times, even to the same person, let alone to different people.

Playlist

Roy C, Shotgun Wedding
Buzzcocks, Breakdown
John Lennon, Mother
Chicago, If You Leave Me Now
T Rex, Children of the Revolution
Blondie, The Tide Is High
Avril Lavigne, GirlFriend
The Turtles, Happy Together
Hazel & Alice, Don't Put Her Down You Helped Put Her There

7

PORNOGRAPHY, AFFAIRS AND OTHER CHALLENGES

Deep Fried America

Alabama, Louisiana, the deep-fried south
Cotton pickin' country, gagging at the mouth
Public virtues are clean and cold
While private vices are mean and sold
Respect your mother
Exploit the sluts
Don't mention bodily parts
Nuts ain't nuts.
Honour childbirth, courage and the flag
But come on the face of the embryonic slag
Her mouth is set in a child-like grin
As the white fluid drips from her mouth to her chin
This is the country of the American dream
Where freedom is a face full of cream

Cream on the cake, the coffee and the fruit
Deep fried America, life is just a root.

Hawaii, 2003

PORNOGRAPHY

As a ten-year old in north London, a child of the '50s,
I shared an interest with my teenage peers for pictures
of naked women and stories about sex. We held a riot-
ous evening in 1954 at the local flea-pit, the Central
Cinema, in College Road, Cheshunt whose somewhat
rotund owner, Mr Carpenter, would, imitating W.G.
Fields, welcome us in by standing in the entrance running his thumbs up and down the inside of his braces
and then twiddling his white handle-bar moustache.
The movie was called *The Garden of Eden** (about a
nudist camp in the US) that had been 'approved' by the
Sunbathers Association of America. Every time a naked-
breasted woman appeared on the screen, we whooped
with delight at such naughtiness, of course, failing to
notice that the naked men were never filmed below the
waist and that the women were restricted to breasts
and buttocks. Children, however, were not restricted in
the way they were filmed, a conceit that underlines the
almost total ignorance of how paedophilia works and
an indifference to its dangers.

Our other sources of naughtiness in the '50s
included *Playboy* and *Health & Efficiency* magazines

---

* https://youtu,be/M2cR5CDf14w

which were discreetly shelved in most newsagents in a section well away from women's magazines such as *Women's Own, My Weekly and Vogue*. It was normal to see 3 o 4 adult males scanning this section but for us teenagers it was 'no boys land'.

A lot of sharing and hiding took place as we made do with what we could scavenge with our bedroom mattresses being the favoured hiding place. This culture persisted until the Internet was on us in the mid-80s. On one delightful visit in 1978 to the elderly parents of a close friend of mine, on the outskirts of Dorking in Surrey, David's father introduced us to the protocols for using the loos. There was a boys' only loo and another one for women. I went to the boys' loo shortly after lunch. It was graced with two piles of the distinctive yellow of National Geographic magazines. I then noticed that one of the piles might have featured in a version of *The Princess and the Pea* fairy story because there was a distorting lump about a third of the way down made by an unexpected intruder. I wiggled it free. Lo and behold, an A5 copy of a girlie magazine, wedged between the yellow, came into view. Obviously, a bit of spice for David's father in his secret room. And a secret I have no doubt he learned as a teenager, way back when.

This environment persisted well into '70s and '80s before, as a porn movie maker might have said, 'après moi le deluge'!

In 2006, when I was a co-founder and chair of the

global digital law start-up *www.leagle.com*, we held a board meeting in Sydney with our colleagues from Australia, the US and India. I had just returned from the UK where, after catching up with my UK children and their offspring, I had been reading a research report on the uses being made of the Internet. Of course, my interest was in the use of online legal materials but the article had a much wider remit than the law. One of its topics was the use of pornography online. I announced to the meeting that this report suggested 80% of all users, men and women, teenagers and seniors, accessed pornography. 'Oh,' said a surprised Mahindra from Bengaluru. 'What do the other 20% do?!'

A good question, Mahindra. The ubiquity of access of pornographic content on the Net is the biggest feature of the Internet's growth, along with media streaming and social media, in the last decade. For my generation, online pornographic content is seen as the exception not the rule. We were used to the analogue world of *Playboy*, *Penthouse* and *Hustler* that I have described above and regard the digital world as transformative and not 'normal'.

I have to come clean at this point. I have been an online user of pornography and like the story about Mahindra, I am sure that I am not in a minority. The motivation is straightforward. It's often highly stimulating material that also shapes and feeds curiosity into the sexual practices of porn stars of all ages, all ethnicities and all social standings. Putting to one side the recent emergence of consensual or ethical pornography there is, of course, no doubt that it is demeaning of the participants and particularly of the women involved but, from some male points of view, this does not seem to make it less exciting. In particular, it is noteworthy that men are often anonymous (wearing masks or acting off camera) unlike the women on show.

There is, however, a transformative aspect in online pornography that seriously disturbs the concerns I am raising in this book for the role of intimacy in ordinary lives. Young men are learning about sex online. Forget the role of teachers like Mary who taught me reproduction biology in 1957 or the playground encounters with teenager girls or joking with boys as to what was 'long and thin, red in parts and goes in tarts?' The Internet offers fast track access to sex destinations which lack a learning process for 'users' and make appalling assumptions about the dynamics and content of sexual intercourse. Active women are described as sluts and whores and active men are pleasure takers without love or care. Many videos champion hardly suppressed abuse and rape without any duty of care for impressionable users, especially young men.

It is clear to me that the nature of the demand for sexual pleasure is very different when you compare men with women. I touched on this in my earlier chapter on the difference between love as a gateway for sex (think men) versus sex as a gateway to love (think women). I appreciate that this distinction does not cover all human beings and I can see that same sex relationships will not share this analysis. But for most heterosexuals, my experience tells me it is so.

A further difference that I have learned is the ways in which orgasm is received. For men it is a mostly decisive short-term need, the drive for which is very difficult to suppress. Once you are on the journey, you won't want to get off until you reach the orgasmic destination. And when you have reached it, depending on your age, after a period of quiet, you are happy to get on board again. I have had periods in my life when I would happily make love every day, maybe twice with a bit of luck.

For women the experience can be very different. There are many women who don't ever get to orgasm, or only very rarely, and for those that do, it is an end in itself that doesn't want to be resuscitated. The needs of my partners over 60 years have been for much less frequency without this suggesting for a moment a lack of love between us.

Pornography aimed at women users does exist but it meets a much smaller demand than that for men. And it must be emphasised that the objectification of women is a tool, if you'll forgive the pun, for an almost total repression of the woman's point of view in all videos. All relationships are pictured as titillation for the male viewer. Whether lesbian or straight, young or old, black or white the alienation of women from the video narratives is complete.

I think it is possible to integrate online access to pornography in a normal heterosexual sex-life but only if it's seen as an extra, a stimulant that does not replace 'the real thing'. This nexus has clearly been crossed when we consider the changing role of Internet sex from the optional extra I have witnessed for people of my age to a living alternative for 'normal' face to face relationships among young males who have never known anything different. These changes have driven the male capacity to make real relationships into the world of Hobbes' *Leviathan* where life is 'nasty, brutish and short'. What this new world is delivering in spades is a loss of innocence. There is a focus on the difference between loving a person for themselves and loving their sex organs for your pleasure. The magic of self-discovery through a tactile relationship with a partner; the way uncertainty drives creativity and the 'she loves me she loves me not' syndrome that bites into your soul with unexpected consequences.

I am not arguing that sex should not be pleasurable and an 'end' in itself. But what porn has done is to remove love-making from its human context – especially by objectifying the role of women into a cycle of behaviours that have nothing to do with love. Porn videos cycle again and again the same actions – strip, suck, submit, semen – and by doing so humiliate women into becoming plastic sex toys. The damage being done may not be particularly harmful for mature male viewers but for teenage and young adult males, porn offers a transformation devoutly to be unwished.

My final word on this topic is that some men see the sex as punishment and the toxic link between sex, invasion, rape and punishment is so evident in porn and equally evident in aspects of everyday life. The US Supreme Court's reversal of a Federal right to abortion in *Roe v Wade* is another example of the regrettable institutionalisation of male power in the sex lives of women.

AFFAIRS AND CHEATING

One of the trickiest things I have had to deal with is the difference between the way I see myself in the world and the ways others see me. Relationships are beset by the different points of view of the protagonists and members of their family and friends. For example, in conversation with a friend (whom I have known for well over 40 years), she described a casual one-nighter of mine, when I was married to Gill, as 'cheating'. The person I had slept with dobbed me in years ago so the event was not 'news'.

Her comments stopped me in my tracks. Over the years I have never described dalliances, short or longer lived, as 'cheating.' I would go so far as to say that seeing the experience from the inside is so different. The event she was referring to was regrettable for all sorts of reasons but 'cheating' wasn't the descriptor that immediately sprang to my mind. 'Stupid', 'heartless' or 'thoughtless' yes but not 'cheating'. But is my response a simple case of denial? That like many men, I carve out a modus operandi in matters of sex to suit my desires rather than squarely confront the moral issues involved?

I'd like to say 'no' but I suspect that I am kidding myself in thinking what the head doesn't know the heart doesn't grieve about, that if you can get away with it then, don't worry, it'll all be alright. As Billy Joel sang, a relationship is a matter of trust and trust as I have argued above only exists as two-way traffic. What this means for me is that provided the values are truly reciprocated in a relationship then it may survive many different ways of conducting it. Thus, arranged and open marriages can work if both parties are 'in it together'. This is a crucial point for success in relationships. Success is not driven by adherence to an external value system like religion, or family life however important they may figure in your make-up. Indeed, the impact of these external influences may be counter-productive by creating repression and guilt. What matters is the shared values of the people involved as laid down between them and how responsive individual behaviours are to them.

Cheating arises when these 'internal' values are ignored or compromised by one partner for their own pleasure or benefit at the expense of the other. Of course, the challenges of managing the different behaviours involved are not equal. Open marriages which became the vogue in the '60s are rarely sustainable despite the shared vision on which they are built. Eventually, the emotional pressures may spin the tryst out of control and the partnership dissolves.

Equally disorienting is the whole process of falling in love – a topic I have covered to an extent in earlier chapters. I have experienced the feeling of being in love (I use the term 'feeling' because there is no external measure of what it is to be in love) five times in my life. Three of these events led to marriages and the two outside marriage were never compatible with that estate. The first of these latter two was a dead-end because my lover, who was older than me, lived a wealthy life style which, as a 23-year-old student, I could never match. Despite the depth of my passion, the idea of getting together was never entertained by me nor I suspect by her either.

Despite this, the impact of this affair on my marriage to Liz was catastrophic. She was now unwillingly displaced in my affections, an outcome from which we never recovered.

The affair meandered along for three or four years, a time during which Liz and I had two more children but, nevertheless, failed to recover the lost ground. The intimacy between us was now hesitant because the damage had been done. I had become vulnerable and there was no doubt that after this I would want to make a change.

I had allowed myself most willingly to be catapulted into a situation that was so destabilising that the collapse of the marriage five years later was inevitable. The fact that I had three children under the age of 10 was never seen by me as a reason for inaction. They weren't seen by me at the time as a reason for staying but rather an issue that breakdown had to accommodate as best it could – a point of view that I guess I inherited from my Dad and about which I would think so differently today.

My second non-marital 'love' relationship took place in Canada where I was regularly travelling on business, a decade or so later. The tap turned on as soon as I landed in Toronto but turned off when I boarded the home-coming plane to Heathrow. The relationship was very special but totally self-contained by geography. The idea of getting together full-time never arose but we enjoyed meeting as and when we could.

The affair ran its course during a very difficult time in my marriage to Gill. It confirms what I have learned about affairs. Whether cause or effect the deception on which they thrive is the enemy of intimacy. What couple-binding won't spring apart when a stray letter, email or SMS revealing the other party involved is accidentally or even furtively discovered? Or, as happened to me to my extreme shame, when their name is unexpectedly referenced by you when making love with your usual partner? After all, cheating does seem to be the right descriptor and I have now added this concept to my list of relevant misbehaviours.

Last but not least, I did have one affair which neither led to marriage nor was grounded by being 'in love'. Nearly 40 years later the woman involved emailed me out of the blue to see how I was getting on. This followed a night when she dreamt about me and strangely she had popped up in my dreams too. All this as I am writing this book.

I sent her a note and enclosed a poem for her to see. She responded 'that's all very well but it's not personal; to me. Can you do any better?' I wrote this new poem for her which I attach below.

Hello!

We met in a distant time
when our marriages were in retreat
workmates in more than one sense
our hearts increasing their beat
The simplicity of our love
as we engaged here and there
a constant reminder
how joyful love is when shared
You were generous and kind
as true lovers often are
I was perhaps more restrained
as you gently raised the bar
Forty years later
on opposite sides of the planet
we share dream-time together
who can explain that?
Here's to you

my flame from the past
it's good to be reminded
how fond memories can last

<small>ROZELLE 2022</small>

ART FOR ART'S SAKE

Sitting close to pornography, among the other challenges, is the history of the sexualisation of women in our culture. This may take the form of things like the treatment of women in visual arts – the religious and bucolic paintings of Venetian painters like Titian, Giorgione, Veronese, and Tintoretto; the adoration of the female body that we see in the works of the 18th and 19th Century painters such as Ingres, Gainsborough and Reynolds and, more recently, the exploration of the forms the female body might take in the works of painters like Picasso, Modigliani, Allen Jones and Lucian Freud.

'Art' photography has also developed its own language for representing the female form in an idealised way as in the work of Man Ray, Bill Henson and Yoosuf Karsh. The cultural artefacts and media that carry these motifs are infinitely varied. We can add poetry (think Byron, Donne and Keats), fiction (how about *Forever Amber, Fifty Shades of Grey* and *American Graffiti?*) advertising (particularly for consumer brands), pop music (especially rap and rock and a special mention for Robert Palmer) and TV & Film (like *The Night Manager, Emmanuelle, The French Lieutenant's Woman*).

It is hard in responding to these cultural matters not to be caught up by the ambiguity of the way adult women and young girls are presented. Just as a feminist critique may focus on the way these art forms disempower women by making them objects of desire so, an equally feminist response will also see the participation of women in these sexual manifestations as being empowering.

At a meeting with a group of enlightened futurists in San Francisco in the mid-'90s, I suggested my favourite quirky book title was an Angus & Robertson tome called *No More Menstrual Cramps and Other Good News*. Well you could have heard a tampon drop. The public mention of sexual bodily function was too much for the group. The prudishness of U.S. culture took over and the embarrassing topic was quickly moved right along.

The public/private divide is critical. For in private, U.S. culture is anything but prudish, hosting as it does the world's leading market for pornography. Prudes in public vs pornographers in private. A legacy, perhaps, from 19th Century Victorian Britain and the liberal philosophy of John Stuart Mill.

The Bill Henson furore in 2012 also nagged away at the interface between art and pornography. My colleague Richard Watson and I wrote a piece for my website *Homepagedaily* that looked at the social implications of the confiscation of his photographic artworks from the Roslyn Oxley gallery in Sydney.

In case you've been living in Canberra or Beaconsfield for far too long, a prude is someone that is uncomfortable with sexuality or other forms of relatively harmless mischief. Prudery is also a term meaning displaying excessive modesty, such as a politician who is uncomfortable with nudity.

On paper Bill Henson is not a prude, but perhaps the rest of us are becoming so.

There was nothing new in the seized Henson artworks – he'd been doing it for years – so that this media storm in a legal teacup clearly demonstrated that while the public likes the splash of paint on canvas it has a crisis of imagination when it comes to photographic images. As one of my sons noted at the time, if Henson had converted the photos into fictionalised images then no one would have bothered.

It is unlikely that the images themselves were the cause of the problem but rather the social confusion which patterns the way we respond to them. And of course parental approval is essential to protect children's well being and privacy. The uncomfortable truth is that these images perfectly reflected back to us in black and white an image of ourselves that we are not comfortable with – that individually and collectively we are suffering from a crisis of confidence about our relationships with children.

A friend recently said he could not take the teenage daughter of one of his friends on a fishing trip without a chaperone for much the same reason. Did you know for example, that unaccompanied adult men are no longer allowed to sit next to unaccompanied children on some aeroplanes?

This is insane and so too is the idea that children's bodies should be covered at all times. One of our baby kids wandered, naked, next door only to return 15 minutes later with a pair of undies donated by concerned neighbours.

Each to their own, of course, but technology is making life much easier for us all to misbehave, but most people are good and if we assume that they aren't what kind of society are we creating for these kids to grow up in?

And what's next? Some years ago, Peter Couchman interviewing US feminist author Marilyn French on ABC Radio expressed his concern that it was no longer possible for a father to bathe his baby daughter for fear of being sued for abuse. Ms French tempered his concern with the simple affirmation that adults always know when they are misbehaving, whatever the law might say about it.

Are naked babies to be banned on Australian beaches and other public spaces? Why stop there? Perhaps in the future politicians will not be allowed to kiss babies on the campaign trail because heaven knows where this activity could lead, both for the politician or the baby. Imagine Australian male prime-minister getting into trouble with his constituents for brushing his lips across a baby girl's cheeks!

But just as all this stuff is happening – surrounded by fears, prudery and passion – we are subscribing to a society in which the experience of childhood is being truncated. The 'lost childhood' devoured by the global media, by advertisers promoting teen sexuality, Internet pornography, by techno gadgetry, image-neurosis (anorexia etc), video games, fast-food and the other dark arts of latter-day commerce.

Henson's work shows us the transient fragility of the innocence of children. As soon as we see his work as being perverse or 'disgusting' the innocence of the child perishes.

SUBJECT/OBJECT/US

Sideways

You always
You never
You should
You don't
You can't
You would

I want
I listen
I try
I love
I need
I fly

We can
We shall
We change
We embrace
We conjoin
We remain

Rozelle 2024

Intimate binary relationships create significant complexities around the status of each party, the one with the other. This is not just a matter of personalities. however large a part they play. There is more to it than the impact of the control freak, jealous partner, hedonist or home lover. What I have in mind is the institution of marriage which houses the actors; the theatre inherited from the past on which the drama of life plays out. Pushing the metaphor, hopefully not too far, these actors on the stage morph between being the subject or object of the play as a result of the focus of the dramatic events in which they participate.

For example, birthing children, business promotion, wealth acquisition, sporting success, illness, ageing and death are the kind of events that continually change the script, our role in it and the way, as a couple, we see each other.

The subject/object switchback is a common feature of all relationships. I can look at my personal story and see how I have moved from one to the other as a result of the formative events I have outlined. This may often be 'for better for worse' but above all it is about the distracting and bumpy path that we tread both socially and emotionally.

When I migrated to Australia, expecting a three-year stay, I left three children in London who were now experiencing me as an absentee dad; an object on another planet and no longer the subject of their daily lives. I had no idea at the time of the transformative effect of my decision to come to Sydney with their step-mother who ironically then moved from subject to object by returning back to the UK with my fourth child. I think my own childhood, despite its critical contribution to my intellectual development, did not nurture emotional intelligence in me because my parents were so pre-occupied with their issues and lacked true experience of how nuclear families operate.

Whereas I see the subject/object as being a common dynamic in all relationships, there is of course a third dynamic which supplants these two and that is 'us'. 'It is hardly surprising, given the focus of this book, that I see 'us' as the transformative dynamic on which intimacy builds. Subject/object dynamics are the stuff on which divorce and separation feed. 'Us' embraces the most powerful world-view – 'it's you and me against the world'.

IDENTITY

Germaine Greer anticipated the social and psychological complexities of gender-typing, identity and roles that have become front-page issues today. The trans-gender debate with J K Rowling arguing that trans-gender claims are weakening the feminist movement and that we need to return to a biological rather than psycho/social definition of 'woman' is but one example. There also seems to be much confusion, today, about distinguishing sex and gender. It seems that we have no choice as to our sex because it is biologically determined but every choice when it comes to defining our gender which is a flexible socio-psychological feature of our lives.

Social behaviours become questionable with the adoption of medical interventions to 'trans' gender for individuals with the time and money to make such changes. It is early days as protagonists are mostly under 40 years old and we don't have sustained case-histories to guide us. I have tracked one or two cases in my circle of family and friends and the over-riding first impression is how unhappy the outcomes can be for those involved. It seems to me that gender fluidity that focuses on make-up and clothing is an option we should not question but that to remove breasts surgically and to change the hormonal diet of a person to help he/she/it move sharply along the gender continuum from M to F or F to M are simply mistakes.

Nothing points more clearly to what's going wrong here than the attack being made on sexist – or is it gender-biased language. We are being told that 'breast feeding' is an unacceptable activity and must be replaced by 'chest-feeding'. Likewise, 'breast-milk' must become 'chest-milk' or 'human-milk' while 'mum' is no longer an appropriate way of describing the milk-providing agent, unless conjoined by '. . . or parent' just so the non-binary gender-neutral reproducer gets a look-in.

I am reminded of some of the silliness generated by the Ms/Miss debate in the '70s but at least that debate was primarily an important clear-cut one about power and not about gender-identity and yielded an appropriate result.

But what really matters to me is the death–knell that this kind of political correctness imposes on our language – on its poetry and social history.

Are we now to correct William Blake's use of the word 'harlot' in his poem *London* to read thus:

'. . . the youthful *sex-worker's* curse'?

Or must Shakespeare's sonnet be rewritten:

'. . . When my love swears that *they are* made of truth/ I do believe *them*, though I know *they lie*,/ That *they* might think me some untutor'd *teenager*,/ Unlearned in the world's false subtleties.'?

Even Rumpole of the Bailey would be caught up in this fiasco of language abuse when his *partner* has to be described as '*them indoors*' or '*they who must be obeyed*'.

Simone de Beauvoir pioneered the idea that biological differences between the sexes were an inalienable differentiator underlying the social and psychological aspects of human development. The recent interest in epigenetics (the way changes in organisms are caused by modification of gene expression rather than alteration of the underlying genetic code itself) has been helpful in trying to resolve the nature/nurture dilemma of the last century. But, it has a long way to go to be resolved as more than an interesting theory. And, even then, its impact on choices taken by an individual is likely to be fuzzy.

My partner (a woman who I will never refer to as 'they'!) has been a practising nurse and midwife for over 40 years. She puts it bluntly. 'Menstruation, rape, pregnancy, childbirth, mothering, sexual abuse, social and economic discrimination, fashion, male chauvinism, menopause, face-lifts, Botox, ageing, home-alone – men don't have to deal with any of these in the way we women do. It's definitely not a level playing field.'

Clearly today the 'male point of view' has not been fully abandoned in favour of gender (sic) equality. As Isobel Allende argues when being interviewed by ABC Radio's Phillip Adams about her memoir The *Soul of a Woman*, we have made progress but we have not done enough. We are still living in a patriarchal society, and not just in Australia but globally. The impact of Muslim fundamentalism in the hands of the Taliban in Afghanistan on the education and social roles of their women defies belief.

There have been improvements, for sure, in role-sharing, especially in raising children, but when push comes to shove, the male partner's responsibilities to his work place usually comes first. This observation is not a matter of theory. It is based on my experience and my behaviour. I was always ready and willing to share domestic duties but nearly always in the context that my work was paramount – an approach still shared by most middle-class dads in my social network. Of course, life-changing events would alter the priorities but the hum-drum day to day assumptions seem to be fairly permanent.

It is depressing how little progress has been made in changing the culture in which women even in western democracies have to operate. One of my three daughters, an academic sociologist researching, for over a decade, family issues at Cambridge University, points out, working women still have responsibility for about 70% of domestic chores despite the dramatic increase in two-income families.

The women's movements of the 70's gave women a new strength to pioneer social change in the workplace and has, even, provided a worldview that encourages men and women to adapt the dynamics of family and work life to new situations. But what is missing 50 years on is any sense of transformation of these dynamics. The preoccupation with #metoo and its targets – men in positions of power abusing their dominant roles to the disadvantage of women – tells us how transformative social change might be in the future but there is such a long way to go.

Social media have exacerbated the complexities of modern life. At the very moment we see signs of progress, regressive features pop up. Female narcissism, for example, has been given full bore by sites such as Facebook and Instagram and has as its most significant 'tool'- the selfie. Every day I am asked to like pics of young women directly or indirectly connected to me, pouting at the camera in sexually alluring poses.

Men and women – even allowing for the complexities of the gender-identity spectrum – are different. Biologically, emotionally, intellectually and socially. There is a general failure of males to recognise that these differences are not there to engender distortions in power as distributed between the sexes. They are there to support the way power is handed out embracing equity, justice, fairness, love and the need for each and every one of us to have the opportunity to lead fulfilling lives.

In the old days of female secretaries supporting male executives, day to day, the patriarchal hierarchy was the organising principle as to who did what and when. I was as complicit as the next man in endorsing the pro-male dynamic despite any protestations I might make as to my values and left of centre world view.

Jenny, my secretary for a time at Granada Publishing in the UK, came into my office nervously handing me her resignation as she was taking up a new position with a small boutique publisher. I didn't fight hard to keep her, so off she went. Six months later I dropped in to see her in her Soho office and was amazed to learn that she had been promoted to the role of publishing manager – basically running the admin for the company across all functions. I had no idea that she would be a candidate for such a job, let alone be good at it and I learned, not for the first time, that I was silently supporting outmoded male-dominated ways of seeing the world.

These assumptions are deep-seated and hard to change. The frustration of women battling against the system is evident in the journey many women make that ends up with their isolation from and resentment of the proffered pathways for careers and family life. It's an uneasy social contract that defeats so many people.

One of the ironies of the way these social contracts work relates to the common experience that women have to live for a decade or so after their partners have shuffled off their mortal coil. My mother was a case in point. When my dad died aged 86, my mum was only 74. She looked exhausted and spent at his funeral. I remember seeing her sitting on the sofa in her Isle of Wight home at the wake and thinking she wasn't going to last long. But she did. She revived and flourished then to live one of the happiest decades of her life, no longer trapped by a man who disempowered her in so many ways.

The marriage contracts which are so prolific in our society are hierarchical in structure and their true nature is only revealed as people are released from them.

Significant transformation in the role of women in our society has not taken place. The glass ceiling, though raised, is still there. Women still have major responsibility for domestic work and in the workforce those domains in which they provide special services – such as nursing, teaching, child and aged care – are poorly paid and do not carry much in the way of social status.

Ironically, the area in which transformation has been evident is gender identity. The journey from Male, Female (whether Miss, Ms, Mrs) to Female, Male, Intersex, Trans, Non-Conforming, Personal, and Eunuch has complexified the very premise on which *The Female Eunuch* was built. In 1970 gender was a matter of objective consideration, usually of the sex organs of the person. Now in 2023 it has become a subjective matter of self-identification. Not what I am but what I want to be. Whatever the virtues may be for this transformative change, it certainly muddies the role of the feminist and women's movement. And old-fashioned patriarchy might just keep on keeping on, largely untroubled by what seems to me to be obfuscating nonsense. Of course, there is a gender spectrum but why do we want to politicise it? There can be no female road to freedom in that kind of world and, yet, the female road to freedom is devoutly to be wished.

I give the last word on this topic to jockey Rachael Blackmore who won the Grand National Steeplechase at Aintree in 2021 aboard Minella Times.

In her first interview on the way to the dismounting enclosure, she was asked what it felt like to be the 'first female' to win the world's most famous horse race. 'I don't feel male or female right now,' she replied. 'I don't even feel human.'

AI AND SOCIAL MEDIA

The impact of technology has been the hallmark of a world in transition since 1900 but none more so in the last 20 than that of IT, social media and artificial intelligence. They are combining to transform the environment in which relationships between human beings takes place.

I was in a coffee shop the other day with ten tables each occupied by one person with their faces buried in a screen. Chatting away both digitally and orally – pleasure and business – some even smiling These changes are not organic or temporary; they are gamechangers without an outcome in sight. We don't have much of a clue where they will take us. This uncertainty makes pontificating about how they will impact on how we relate to each other extremely difficult but it does beg for me the question – is human nature a constant? Is the content of intimacy unchanging over time whatever the technological and other provocations may deliver?

Anyone who loves the poetry of Shakespeare will line up in the camp of the universal existence of an unchanging human nature. Followers of another writer, William

Gibson, will head for the transformational camp. 'Plus les choses changent, plus elles sont différentes'.

I think the jury is out on this debate and likely to stay out for some time. The sheer quantitative aspect of the human reach of social media combined with the debilitating affect of AI on political integrity and truth are likely to put future relationships under pressures we have not had to handle thus far. Imagine the world of Jane Austen with Instagram, Tiktok, YouTube, Facebook and WhatsApp among the frontline channels for communication and acting out of sense, pride, prejudice and sensibility. Or Sydney Carton working out ethical standards for action in French revolutionary Europe with the network of news providers who jostle for our attention today. Who should he believe?

My intuitive response to the question about human nature is indicated in this poem.

Big Picture Blues

Telling
We need the big picture
to better understand
the mountains and valleys
the lay of the land
The geology of the present
asks us to be aware;
the journey we have made
and how we got there

But life's experience
is not general
nor public nor wide
It's something ephemeral.
Join with me,
let's get vocal,
for our lives are narrow
private, and local.

Showing
Your body warmth
flows into mine
sharing this space
for a moment in time
Fleetingly we kiss
and cuddle
blissfully aware
life is a muddle.

Holding your hand,
I feel joined
to a permanent
other of value uncoined
In this sea of dreams
life is a mystery
unconnected to
a big picture history.

My experience is that intimacy is a private event unchanged by the environment in which it operates; that my experience is special and cannot be meaningfully shared other than with my partner in crime. The fabric of society will continue to change year on year but the value of intimacy is undaunted.

Playlist

. . . .

Kings of Leon, Sex on Fire
The Motels, Porn Reggae
The Cure, Pornography
Rihanna, Sex with Me
Sex on the Internet, Girl and Girl
Don Maclean, American Pie
Billy Joel, A Matter of Trust
Taylor Swift, Illicit Affairs
Joni Mitchell, A Case of You
Harry Styles, Fine Line
Robert Palmer, Addicted to Love
The Beatles, Dear Prudence
Joan Osborne, Let's Just Get Naked
Chelsea Cutler, I Choose Crying Over You
Kinks, Lola
Johnny Tillotson, Poetry in Motion
Marianne Faithful, The Ballad of Lucy Jordan
The Cure, Pictures of You
Melissa Manchester, Working Girl
Cher, Woman's World
Ladysmith Black Mambazo, We Are One
Helen Reddy, You and Me Against the World

8

FAMILY LIFE

When You've Gone

"When you've gone, so sorry,
OP Shops's won't know themselves
All that crap from your bathroom
And cluttering from the shelves.
"I'll have wall-space to spare
Get rid of those chairs
Stretch out in my bed
Sleep restfully without care
"When you've gone, so sorry
I'll have a ball; not yours of course
But doing my own thing
Painting en plein air, for me the birds still sing
"I'll miss you a little
But not the gambling and races
The knife edge of money
Or the frenetic filled spaces
"When you've gone, so sorry"

BALMAIN, 2016

Since 1970 we can trace two significant economic changes affecting women. There are more two-income families than ever before. Economic pressures have moved the stay at home mothers back into the workforce so escalating house prices are more affordable though still out of reach for many. Two-income households are now the norm and not the exception. Superannuation has been increased significantly, too, building the level of savings in the community to a new high. So far so good, but the reality for families with children is at the very moment of procreation any advances in the status of women regarding equal compensation with their male counterparts, head south at a rate of knots.

Gross salaries and super may be preserved during maternity leave but, thereafter, go to zero until the mother returns to the workforce. And when she does her gross wages are impacted by the cost of childcare which may make her net income have little by way of a surplus that contributes much to the family budget. Women lose out again as the two-stroke economy continues to increase the income gap between men and women.

Look at the people at any institution in contemporary Australia and the dominance of male representation is still there. Whether a deck of cabinet ministers, the advisory board for a university, the 'casa nostra' of the directors of a major corporation — it's men, men all the way down. As has been revealed in the recent documentary (*Msrepresentation*) on the role of women in the Australian parliament, not only are the numbers skewed in favour of males but the content of legislative debates about women's rights (abortion, abuse, discrimination and pay) are acted out male to male. Things continue to improve on the numerical front but it's still a male-dominated sanctuary where legislative shape is given to our democracy.

As I write, the level of anger being felt by women is rising. Whether its source is rape, physical abuse, mental cruelty – women are voicing their deep disquiet with the world they are born into and demanding change. Carpe diem! As Julia Jacklin sings, 'I don't want to be touched all the time, I raised my body up to be mine.' Institutionalised men do not know what to do about it. They may see the rationale behind the anger but cannot separate the ethics of what should follow from the politics that caused it. I have no doubt that it is the politics of gender in our society that should be the target for change.

The problem with this topic, as I have argued throughout, is changing gender politics is not just a matter of behaviour. It is equally a systemic problem which inhabits the ways in which men see the world, how those beliefs are nurtured by organisations such as the church, education, the nuclear family, the military and representative politics. Behavioural change will not flip the switch without, first, deep change of the social and institutional culture. After all is said and done, dear chicken, the henhouse came first!

The politics of institutional change are complex. I could theorise about these complexities but feel drawn back to what I have learned in very specific circumstances about family life. I have lived in three nuclear families in each of which at least four of my seven children share only one of the parents. The layering has now been embellished by 17 grandchildren resident in six nuclear families equally divided between Australia and the UK. The mathematics of the number of prime and ancillary binary relationships this group is supporting are beyond me but calculable if you have got the time. There are hundreds.

The first learning I have made from this is the mind-boggling complexity of the relationship dynamics whose interactions create the family as a working system. This topic has engaged creative writers and filmmakers as much as it has therapists of various kinds. And there is no doubt that the accepted nuclear family dynamic has been under deep scrutiny and continuous pressure for over half a century. From RD Laing (author of *The Divided Self*) and Ken Loach (*Family Life*) to Jonathan Franzen (*The Corrections*) and Robert Redford (*Ordinary People*) – not to mention Toni Morrison (*Beloved*), Joanna Trollope (*The Rector's Wife*) and Liane Moriarty (*The Husband's Secret*) – it's game-on for young and old, male and female.

The fragility of nuclear family dynamics has, perhaps, been best expressed by my experience across three marriages of how attendance makes such a difference.

It goes like this. When everyone is on hand, the family feels as if it is at the point of collapse. This is caused, as far as I can tell, by the freezing of the relationships outlined at the beginning of this chapter. As family members we each bring to the table a fixed set of relationships with each other and the world view that comes along with it.

We are definitely not for turning as the role play is acted out perfectly by each of us. These tableaux often feel like the end of the world is nigh but there is a miraculous variation close at hand. Remove any one family member from the nuclear family scene (Dad flying off to Asia; Mum playing hockey in Melbourne; daughter on a school trip to the Southern Highlands; son on a scout trip to Darwin) and these preconceptions melt away and a new order is enjoyed by all.

Parents also tend to sustain their views of family life by fixing the way they see their children after the family has adjusted to the children leaving home. How often did my heart sink when, though originally looking forward to visiting my parents, as I rang their front door bell. I was suddenly a 14-year-old rebellious teenager again.

Participating in an extended family, as I have done since 1974, changes things dramatically. The private intimacy of the original nuclear family is broken and the relationships are redrawn to accommodate new adult members (partners, their grown-up kids, their parents and friends), step-children and any new children borne to the new pairings.

Distractions

Oh yes I have many distractions
With babies down-under galore,
A wonderful partner to be with
Three children living almost next door.
It's now fifty years since
My Tabby first came to be
To join gentle Sam, sweet Liz and bright Tom
And the soon to be errant me.
Each day I return to that moment
and wish that I could put it right
But life's wheels have carried on turning
As darkness replaces the light
Not everything is lost, however
Waves lap on a different shore.
My glorious seventeen grand-children
Played no part in what went before.

ROZELLE, 2022

My first nuclear family comprised the five of us. My second just three and my third five again. But measured cumulatively, as one extended family, the numbers, including my kids partners and my grandchildren, are nine, thirteen, and something around forty, respectively.

Our family life is rich and by dint of the numbers, unmanageable. What we have lost as a result of broken marriages (the absolute trust at least one of us expected to remain), we have gained from the diversity and size of the group. There is really something for everyone somewhere. And in particular the Australian dimension offers UK members an avenue to new experiences and vice-versa.

As far as extended families go, we have become really good at it. This is not down to any one person but because we have all tried to make a second-best situation as good as it might be. We like each other and enjoy being together as and when we can. It is ironic that the distance between some members may, in fact, promote rather than hinder harmony. But we need to be careful not to argue that the ends justify the means. I do believe in the value of the nuclear family and I deeply regret having been, for Liz, a destructive force on that score.

What are the other components of a successful extended family? The first is time. The moment of relationship breakdown is usually one where emotions are out of control as the game of life is disrupted by the veritable spanner in the works. Passions run high, allegiances among family and friends are disrupted and on occasion are never to be mended. However, time is of the essence. And in my experience, it takes two or three years for the new model to settle down and be in place, whichever side you are on. But settle it will so much so that, when you are comfortable with the hand that has been dealt, you may reflect on the lost relationship in comparative rather than absolute terms.

The second is patience. Allow things to unravel

and rewind according to determinants that you don't control. What I mean is that the protagonists in a breakdown tend to be used to the idea of being in control. When I left Liz all those years ago it never occurred to me that I could have done otherwise but when I did leave I was sensible enough to be patient with those affected by it all not to try and control their responses.

When Gill and I broke up, I was lucky enough to meet Susie soon after – yes two weeks, I know, how lucky can you be! We met in May at a birthday party dinner for my friend Greg, in Giardinetto's restaurant in Crown Street, Sydney. We moved in together just five months later on the ground floor apartment of *The Castle* – a grand sandstone folly at the City end of Raglan Street, Mosman.

Susie's parents were understandably less than impressed with my CV. Two wives, four children, no assets – and a pommy 'bath-dodger' to boot. They refused contact and would stay at *The Castle's* portcullis rather than venture in. My strategy was not to engage in a fight for recognition but to display in our actions how much Susie and I loved each other. Sure enough, after about a year of gentle diplomacy, the tables turned and I was promoted to favoured son, in a house full of women, for evermore.

I think the next practical contribution relates to managing the changing relationships with your children from a previous relationship. The first and commonest hurdles are the relationships between the step-parents and their newly acquired step-children. The immediate problem is the crystallisation of attitudes at the very beginning of these relationships. The step-child feels they have been sold short and they miss the departing parent. It's almost impossible to sort these matters out however hard the step-parent tries. The age of the kids is not a key variable although it's a tougher problem with teenagers than toddlers. As Gill once described it, you end up in a lose-lose. You lose because you are not the mother of the children but at the same time you are being asked to provide motherly services. You lose again because the child does not easily recognise the emotional content of these motherly services. Thanks are not easily won.

These are intractable problems which we have worked through, every now and then, as best we can. Despite the ruffles, our extended family relationships are in good shape mainly, I think, because we have not made of these difficulties mountains to climb. Love and quietude are the key.

One advantage of the extended family is that, as parents, when the 'steps' are involved the proprietorial aspects of family relationships are diminished. What I mean is that our 'ownership' of our children and the behaviours that go along with that sense are weakened.

The idea of a trade whereby we provide sustenance and security which our children return by seeking to fulfil our expectations for them, loses its relevance. As my Dad once said, the only responsibility you have for your children is to their physical protection and emotional health but nothing more.

Sibelius

I am listening to
His 4th Symphony
Which floods my mind
With memories of us
As young kids
Not always unkind

I hope you still
remember
The mushroom soup
Gin and Dubonnet
And bicycle rides
On Shalden Hill
Watching Tom
In the wheatfield
Sam and his fish fingers
Tabby la tantrum
And that picnic
On the way to Stratford
Life can be cruel
We easily forget
The pleasures that make us
Followed by pain

As we go over the bad bits
Again and again
I want you to know
That deep in my heart
Is your special place
We are quiet and secure
Enjoying what we had
Though it would not endure

ROZELLE, 2019

In my experience, the idea that children have a 'performance-duty' owed to their parents, is counter-productive. In the same way, expectations can backfire as was the case with my brother Dan. My parents got a bee in their bonnet that he was cut out to follow his love of nature and particularly feathered birds by pursuing natural history as his reason for being. Dan disagreed and went out of his way to reject academically their version of his what he should do. It all went wrong when he failed his 'A' Levels to find himself facing an uncertain future.

But he got a job at the Natural History Museum in South Ken and a few years later found himself as a team member on a bird collecting expedition to North West Australia. This was followed by a stint in Kenya helping with safaris before applying to do as science degree at Oxford. Ten years almost to the day he crashed his A levels saw Dan as a mature student at Oxford doing the subjects he had rejected ten years ago.

The learning I take form this story is not to blame my parents for their encouragement of Dan's 'hidden' interest but to add to the idea of intimacy that, at the family level, it is an understanding of the fragile nature of the relationships within the family and the need to do less rather than more to promote them. Intimacy between parents and children is as implicit, warm and malleable as it is between the parents themselves. It is not explicit, cool and rigid.

The idea that as parents we are there to create a moral compass for our children is fraught with difficulties. It is not our job to insist on moral behaviours but we do want to draw boundaries beyond which we do not expect them to go. Drugs, racism, kindness, are just some of these areas and, once more, painting a picture of do's and don'ts is best done in an implicit way by example rather than lecturing the wee bairns on what gives and what doesn't.

Expectations are the bugbear of parenthood. Of course, we want our children to be successful achievers of one kind or another but the essential focus is on achieving for themselves and not for others. Private secondary education exemplifies this crux.

It's a quick journey from buying the best education you can afford for your kids as a cultural choice to one which is about buying social advantage for them which they had better respect as a trade between us and them. I reckon about 50% of kids who achieve private school success end up in jobs and work environments that are not fulfilling – that is if they haven't already dropped out of university.

Private school education hot-houses do not do your children any favours. At the same time, they magnify social divisiveness and repress independent creativity. I appreciate an aspect of hypocrisy here as I went from a state school to Oxford and had a great time in the City of Spires but I do feel my schooling was undertaken in an environment much like the world I moved on to after tertiary education.

The message from my reflections on family life and intimacy is that they work best when love rather than achievement is the drug and where children are encouraged to find their own pathway to their adult futures.

It is evidence of this that my seven children comprise a university professor, an art teacher and sculptor, a scholarly researcher, a business start-up director, a carpenter/builder, a rock star and an architect.

Our family experience thrives on generosity of spirit, with occasional bitching of course, and the focus on 'wants' rather than 'oughts'.

I captured aspects of this in my recent poem on babies.

Ode to Babies

Life is complex
brutish and short
but it's not like this
on day one.
The world of the baby
simple and pure
sticking out a folded tongue
an amusing lure
Shaking a key ring
banging a spoon
preceding Mozart
when it comes to a tune.
Those eyes so direct
and magical smile
dismantling the
barriers to love.
Arms and legs
like Michelin tyres
as a voice before speech
makes a gurgling sound.
This is life prior to poetry
before music can be formed
yet in every way equal
as so-called progress dawns.

ROZELLE, 2023

Playlist

ABBA, Mama Mia
Julia Jacklin, Head Alone
Neil Young, Already One
Biob Dylan, Forever Young
Lighthouse Family, High
Sly and the Family Stone, It's a Family Affair
Gizelle Smith, Working Woman
Colin Davis, Sibelius 4th Symphony
Travelling Wilburys, Handle Me with Care
Magdalen College, Oxford, Church Bells
The Beatles, She's Leaving Home
John Lennon, Beautiful Boy
Ed Sheeran, Small Bump
Cilla Black, What's it all about Alfie?

9

INTIMACY

The journey I have been on has not in any way been one to test a particular attitude or approach to life. My reasoning is resolutely inductive and captured by the idea that we live our lives in order to learn how to live the life already lived. This is life-long learning in action. It makes us vulnerable to change, as we flip-flop from protagonist to antagonist in a continuously provocative purpose. 'What's it all about, Alfie,' indeed.

We may well treasure the outcomes from the learning treadmill, but, ironically, life-long learning is a bit of a millstone. It assumes there is no such place as a destination. We never reach the buffers at the end of the track because we are always learning new ways of defining where we are going, who we are going with and how, and what the buffers might look like when we get there. A delightful graffiti I saw in the '70s makes the same point. It was written on a British Rail poster in London tube station, advertising, with a courting couple arm in arm on a moonlit platform, that 'the last train leaves later than you think.' The graffiti said 'Why pick on the last train?'!

This account of my life's train journey has interwoven three themes. The first is what happened to me in my love-life presented not always chronologically but certainly in an autobiographical mode. I am humbly indebted to my family fellow travellers who are aware of what I have been trying to do and I do not wish to offend in any way. They have on occasion pulled the 'stop' cord, with justification as I look back.

This quest has also unearthed some of the broad events and people that have shaped my emotional and intellectual life – from friends to writers, philosophers and artists that I have studied or read. I have tried to avoid seeing these players as causes or solutions of my challenges in the strong belief that, like it or not, we are each responsible for our own lives and should not attempt to hide behind other forces out of our control and shaping the environment in which we each live.

The second contrasting theme has been a discussion of the 'big picture' flowing from the first theme, as I try to analyse the particular social settings in which my love-life operates, over time and in different cultural settings. One limitation of the 'big picture' point of view is that it can muddy the relationship between you and your own life by provoking a misunderstanding of what is important because it lies to some extent outside your experience. Can I really understand the impact of social commentators like Germaine Greer, psychiatrists R D Laing and Carl Jung, anthropologist Mary Douglas on the way I have lived my life and the opportunities that I have actually taken (as opposed to those suggested), but which I have allowed to pass by?

My autobiography and the big picture in which it has unfolded together point towards the third theme which is to consider the true nature of intimacy as it is revealed in our love and sexual relationships with each other. I have taken some time to suggest that intimacy is not just about sex and is not just about love but rather the combination of the two. And it is a combination that sees these two 'states' as being symbiotic with each other rather than one taking priority or leading to the other.

My belief in the collaborative nature of true intimacy has an ironic outcome. It kicks the big picture approach to living off the playing field. There is nothing worse in my book than living a 'big picture' life. At the centre of such a universe lies an inflexible morality where every step is taken in the context of what the picture says is right and wrong. When my first marriage went belly-up my dearest close friend, Bernie (an academic psychologist), shrugged his shoulders and remarked, 'I suppose people do what they want to do.' Desire, thus, has a critical influence on our behaviour but the focus of desire is never general but always specific. The big picture does not feature in this romcom but the focus of your affection surely does. This focus is private, narrow and local but it, nevertheless, often feels like it is public, wide and general.

The small things that constitute an intimate life prove that familiarity breeds content. And that familiarity cannot be broken. Every example of the things you share at any moment with each other is alluvial as layer upon layer strengthen the foundation of your relationship. You don't get fazed by the dad-jokes or puns, by the apologies for the same old meal or the failure to put all the laundry in the bin. All these little events conspire to make the journey worthwhile, even though the 'worth' is little.

Looking back on that fateful meeting at the *Spanish Club* over half a century ago with *The Female Eunuch* rattling my cage and my blissful ignorance as to what was to come, I am struck by the role that luck has played in my life. I have been sensitive to social and environmental changes but accept that we cannot control many of the fomatives influences on the way we live and the way life unfolds.

If I were in Swallow Street again but now an octogenarian, what would I be saying to a young hopeful Oliver sitting at the same table trying to reconcile gender and identity politics with artificial intelligence, environmental sustainability, globalisation and social media? I expect I would ring some traditional bells as it is my belief that human nature does not change over time.

—

I have already argued that intimacy is not a destination. It is not William Blake's 'palace of wisdom', however reached but more like Andrew Marvel's collaborative invitation 'come live with me and be my love.'

This poem I wrote for Susie sums it up for me.

Intimacy

Intimacy is your grey-green eyes flashing
    their hooded secret to me
Down the length of this shopping
    mall, competing so easily
With the neon logos that it's a lay down misère.
And it is the curls of the hair on your neck at dawn
As you sleep in the bed, for forty years-a-share.

Intimacy is your generous and 'slightly
    undisciplined' mouth
Outlining the words 'I love you' as you
    hang clothes on the line,
Trousers from the waist, socks toe by toe.
And it is the lambent warmth of your tongue
As you snuggle into my neck, the day's work done.
Intimacy is your warm telephone voice
    bathing my ear in Beijing
As 1.3 billion people strive to make things better
In a dangerous world, taking on the
    ministers of the dead.

And it is the frozen stride which, in your pyjamas,
Your legs have taken, your hands cradling your head.

Intimacy is both your laughter and your tears,
Rejoicing in a joke about a duck going into a pub,
Or contemplating the slow decline of
    your dad in his Hornsby home.
And it is your stooping figure in our garden, shaking
A pulled tussock of grass, and filling
    the air with loam

Intimacy is the gift you have given me
A treasure replacing pearls and diamonds
Simplicity replacing the complex
Making sense of sense making
And making sense of me.

On this your birthday, take this poem, and turn it
Into something which for you means
Intimacy.

ROZELLE, 2016

Playlist

London Grammar, Big Picture
Nik Kershaw, These Little Things
Fairground Attraction, Perfect
Nick Cave, Into My Arms

ACKNOWLEDGMENTS

The inspiration to write this book emerged in 2020, on the 50th anniversary of the publication of *The Female Eunuch* for whose publishing team I was the hardback sales manager for Granada Publishing in London. Jim Reynolds and Sonny Mehta were the most important supporters of my efforts in that role.

Clearly the women in my life have had a huge influence on me and the content of my book for which the three women who graced me with marriage and children – Liz Cornwell, Gillian Lloyd and Susie Brew – have been the most important. They have together enabled our little group to create an apparently successful extended family, despite the inevitable pain and passion, for which my eternal and warmest thanks. They have, also, been kind enough to read the later draft of my manuscript and to provide comments which I have responded to and incorporated in the final version.

My thanks too to my seven children, Tom, Sam, Tabby, Georgia, Harry, Jack and Lily for their love and perseverance on what at times has been a bumpy ride and to their partners and the 17 beautiful grand-children they have produced together.

I would also like to thank the members of the Boys Own Writers' Group in Sydney – particularly Andrew Pesce, Oliver Greeves, Stephen Badger and Walter McIntosh – who have travelled the writing journey with me and provided input for me, especially on trying to balance the 'big picture' aspects of my story with the personal experiences that I have had on the way. And my poetry group, New Voices, run so well by Dexter Dunphy and Rosalie Fishman, has been a wonderful critic of my poetry, some of which finds its way here.

I also owe a special debt to the friends and colleagues who have commented on my book; acts of encouragement and friendship which I treasure.

Last my thanks to Matt Jackson who pioneered for me the use of poetry as an integral part of a prose narrative in the book I published for him in 2016 – *The Age of Affect.*

Wendy McCarthy has been a close ally for the last half-century and has written a foreword for my book that I will treasure.

David Henley and Jon MacDonald have done a wonderful job at Brio Books in giving my book a real presence in a complex world.

And my warmest. thanks to Debbie Lee for Ginninderra Press picking up the book when Brio ran into trouble and for Graham Davidson who has managed the final proofing steps so well.

AUTHOR'S NOTES

I have included poems by me throughout because they were, mostly, written at the time and capture some of the emotions and topics that the book is seeking to address. I have also added playlists throughout of the music that for me has a similar referential role as the poems. Last but not least my family members are all referred to with their real names but I have used pseud-onyms for some of the other participants to preserve their privacy.

'You can tell a lot about a person by what's on their playlist.' Dan to Greta in the movie *Begin Again.*

A VERY SHORT BIBLIOGRAPHY

John Armstrong *Conditions of Love: the Philosophy of Intimacy*

Simone de Beauvoir *The Second Sex*

Andrea Dworkin *Pornography: Men Possessing Women*

Gustave Flaubert *Madame Bovary*

Michael Frayn *Spies*

Germaine Greer *The Female Eunuch*

James Hollis *The Eden Project: In Search of the Magical Other*

Robert Hughes *The Shock of the New*

Matt Jackson *The Age of Affect*

Kate Legge *Infidelity and Other Affairs*

Ian McEwan *On Chesil Beach*

Caitlin Moran *What About Men?*

Virginia Nicholson *Among the Bohemians*

Grahame Swift *Mothering Sunday*

Leo Tolstoy *Anna Karenina*

John Updike *Couples*
Oscar Wilde *A Picture of Dorian Gray*
... and the poetry of, among many, John Keats,
William Wordsworth, T S Eliot, Andrew Marvel,
John Milton, John Donne, William Blake, Gerad
Manly Hopkins, William Shakespeare, Emily
Dickinson, Seamus Heaney, Sylvia Plath and Ted
Hughes.

ABOUT THE AUTHOR

Oliver Freeman has MAs from the Universities of Oxford and Essex where he studied Politics Philosophy and Economics and the Sociology of Literature respectively. He is past chairman of Publish Australia, the Copyright Agency Limited, Viscopy and UNSW Press. He is a also past Vice President/Vice Chairman of the Australian Publishers Association and the Australian Business Foundation.

He started in the publishing profession in 1967 with McGraw Hill in the UK. Then he moved to Granada Publishing in its heyday. His publishing career rattled along and he has been Managing Director of various entities since 1978 and of his own companies (Prospect Media and Richmond Publishing) since moving to Sydney in 1983. He is a bit of an internet entrepreneur – co-founding ebooks.com in 1998; leagle.com in 2005; homepagedaily. com in 2006 and the larrikinpost.com in 2012.

He is also a futurist, founding – with the late Richard Neville – the Neville Freeman Agency in 1992 and working as an Adjunct Professor and Industry Professorial Fellow in the UTS Business School for the last twenty years.

Other than his lifelong interest in poetry, Oliver has written many general non-fiction articles and a first book, *FutureVision Scenarios for the World in 2040*, co-authored with Richard Watson, that was published by Scribe in Melbourne and London. He was also the author of *Cheap Eats in Sydney* from 1985 to 1990.

Last but not least, Oliver has seven children, from three marriages, and, at the time of this publication, 17 grandchildren.

QUOTES FROM PEOPLE WHO HAVE READ ALL OR PARTS OF THE BOOK.

'A member of the team that first published *The Female Eunuch* now writes a book for all male Eunuchs, those in danger of castration by #metoo and other movements. Although many men of his age can still cherish the idea of love, they tend increasingly to add, along with (King) Charles, "whatever love is." This book shows how men can achieve it, with compassion, intimacy and empathy.' – Geoffrey Robertson, QC, Barrister

'A tender meditation on the interplay between kindness, self-care, and connectedness. A lifetime in the making, deeply intimate in the telling.' – Michael Green SC, Barrister

"A piercing and unashamedly personal exploration into the vital topic of male intimacy. Through reflections on his relationship successes and failures, Oliver Freeman has had the strength, insight and wisdom to reflect and share with a rare honesty." – Adam Moxon Simpson, Director, Simpsons Lawyers

"As a futurist Freeman has cut his teeth on creating communal sense from individual behaviour. Now he brings takes the big picture of relationships and posits how it relates to the individual. A must read"– Andrew Pesce, Obstetrician and former President of the Australian Medical Association

'I touched the man's hand and kept it there while he talked. That he was paralysed and had no choice about the contact did not occur to me – what he was saying was so intimate and profound. This was Superman, Christopher Reeve, after his accident. He was describing his predicament and his extraordinary love of science. I knew then but have confirmed since that he was always thus. If only more of us determined alphas could be real supermen, gentlemen, with the gift of intimacy. Oliver's book is a brilliant idea and reminds me how rarely men have really personal conversations with each other.' – Robyn Williams, *The Science Show*

'Intimacy comes in many guises––in a glance, a look, in the holding of a hand––although the concept of intimacy, to some men, means purely sex. Obviously, there is nothing wrong with sex, however the #MeToo movement has brung to light that some men's understanding of intimacy is limited and this limitation may be partly responsible for the way that some men view women, sex and themselves. I believe a book written on this topic by a man, is a book worth writing – and definitely worth reading.' – Ali Whitelock, Poet

'A bold and brave account of making and breaking families from before the sexual revolution of the '60s to the era of "Me Too" told from a male perspective.' – Professor Susan Golombok, Director, Centre for Family Research, University of Cambridge

'Our Boys Own Writers' Group was midwife to Oliver's work on intimacy. We listened, debated and laughed at the anecdotes and reflections. Better still we asked ourselves questions about our own relationships and realised we should do so more often.' – Oliver Greeves, Writer

'How can men and women so differently express what love means to them? The romantic novel is not an anomaly – girls grow up with a notion of true love and fundamentally believe in it. Could it be that males do not understand that romantic notion and women, in turn, do not see that the sex drive, even domination, is a lead motivator for many men? I don't know the answer to these questions. Oliver Freeman's quest to explore intimacy in a relationship will certainly help me with this puzzle.' – Susan Oliver, Chair, The Wheeler Centre, Melbourne

'If there is a person to write this story – which captures not only the ark of a single man's life, and its web of deeply transformative relationships and intimacies, but also, of course, the radical changes to the institutions of marriage and the expectations made of men as they age – it is Oliver. There are so many men I'd love to recommend this book to. The world needs this book, I'm sure it will be a better place for it.' – Sarah Barns, Consultant

'This book is overdue by generations and Oliver Freeman is the person who can delve into this area for men. To heal and to believe.' – Dr Bronwyn Bancroft, Artist

'Intimacy is that delicate and unexpected visitor that creeps up on you and gently enters your soul after a lifetime of shared joys and some suffering, of authentic humility, of self-reflection and corrugated-iron honesty. The joy of intimacy is purchased at a price – and you have to be prepared to pay it - and the price is a willingness to listen, to value another person's dignity and independence, to be honest with oneself and humble in the presence of the other. Oliver shares his views about intimacy as a destination and opens his heart to telling us about the journey.' – Chris Geraghty, Former Judge and Priest

'Men have, on the whole, attempted intimacy as if it were a novel, and they, its hero. Too many have wound up as the villain or the fool. There always was more to it – to loving and being loved – than the badly written melodramas we took as our scripts. We tried to steal the show when what was wanted was that we turn up in our lives. Presence, not stardom. What we overlooked was poetry. The poetics of being – the art of being with. The lyric way – of life and love – is made of moments and layers and complexity and mystery and depth and transcendence of self. To live lyrically is to live, as Jane Hirshfield puts it, awake to your connections—one Being profoundly connected to a whole ecology of affection. Intimacy is not something you do, in other words; it's something you are. It is a Being-With that no amorous adventure, no love story, can even get you near. A good marriage, the poet Rilke tells the young poet, is a "marvellous living side-by-side", in which each entrusts the other to be the custodian of his or her solitude. Each of us in a marriage then world work to nourish and defend, not our own coming into self-hood, but the others. How a man might do that is what Oliver tells us here. Intimacy without poetry is a singer without a song. And Oliver Freeman knows it. It's what he's saying here in this guidebook to the poetics of connection, and half of how he says it is in verse. In the poems of his own that Oli includes here, he enacts what any man who wants intimacy must learn the courage to attempt: vulnerability. To himself, to the intimate other, to the world.' – Mark Tredinnick, Poet

'To illustrate this narrative of his search for intimacy, Oliver includes a number of his own poems. Some were written at important times in the evolution of a relationship while others are subsequent reflections. To quote a line from one of these poems, they are "archives of remembering", that provide another source of succinct insights into how his understanding of intimacy developed.' – Dexter Dunphy AM, Poet and Emeritus Professor

'From a childhood and adolescence lacking in examples of intimacy, he traces his experiences in relationships through the freedom of the '60s, the feminist movement and his several marriages to the #MeToo movement.' – Jennifer Thurstun, Poet and Linguist

'At a critical phase of shifting relationships between the sexes, Oliver provides important and engaging insights on how men – and women – can achieve true intimacy.'– Ross Dawson, Futurist, Author and Keynote Speaker